Acknowledgements

The depth of Ayr United's history can be compared to a bottomless pit. That is why so many books have been extracted from the material meticulously gleaned from the archives. It would be a pointless exercise to compile research notes with no outlet. Each new book comes from the seed of an idea that ultimately proves workable.

Illustrative material is altogether different. I have successfully amassed an extensive collection of vintage Ayr United photographs but it is challenging to find ones which remain unseen or rarely seen.

Gary Halliday, I thank you for permitting me to use the cache of photographs which fell precisely into this category, including the oldest known Ayr United team picture.

I have a boyhood memory of grown-up Ayr United fans talking about 'old Mr Moffat'. He served on the board from 1923 until 1965 and by the 1960s it is doubtful whether anyone at Somerset Park could recall the days of his youth. Gordon McCreath has kindly supplied a photo to prove that, contrary to popular belief, Mr Moffat was indeed young once! The image of him in an Irvine Meadow team group from 1898 is simply splendid.

113 years later Mark Roberts was involuntarily floored at Brechin. David Sargent captured the incident to perfection and I am grateful for his permission to use the image.

I am equally grateful for the use of photos taken by Brian Caldwell and those from the archives of the *Ayrshire Post*.

Graeme Miller, I am indebted to you for permitting me to use your photograph of Ian McCall.

Both the *Ayrshire Post* and the *Ayr Advertiser* are to be congratulated for their unashamed Ayr United bias, right from the foundation in 1910. I have taken great delight in including contemporary quotes, many of which display the incontestable fact that the journalists had a passion for the club.

A little less delight has been taken in publishing the fact that Ayr United did not come good for a £500 debt to Preston North End in 1939! This snippet came from their club historian Ian Rigby. Luckily it was written off.

The final acknowledgement goes to the work done by the succession of Ayr United managers through the years. Sometimes their efforts were in vain. Sometimes it came to glorious fruition. Either way it is all chronicled here.

Duncan Carmichael
Monkton, Ayrshire.
August 2017.

Ayr United F.C. Managers

Also by Duncan Carmichael:

Official History of Ayr United Football Club Volume 1 –
    Contour Press 1990.
Official History of Ayr United Football Club Volume 2 –
    Contour Press 1992.
Images of Sport – Ayr United FC – *Tempus 2001.*
Ayr United Classics – *Tempus 2002.*
100 Ayr United Greats – *Tempus 2004.*
Walking Down the Somerset Road – *Fort Publishing 2006.*
Ayr United Miscellany – *Amberley Publishing 2011.*
Ayr United At War – *Mansion Field 2014.*
Ayr United On This Day – *Kennedy & Boyd 2016.*

Ayr United F.C. Managers

Duncan Carmichael

Kennedy & Boyd

Kennedy & Boyd
an imprint of
Zeticula Ltd
Unit 13
196 Rose Street
Edinburgh
EH2 4AT
Scotland

http://www.kennedyandboyd.co.uk
admin@kennedyandboyd.co.uk

First published in 2017

Copyright © Duncan Carmichael 2017
Cover design © Zeticula Ltd 2017

ISBN 978-1-84921-165-9

Contents

Illustrations

Introduction

The role of the football manager has changed radically since 1910. It is inconceivable in the modern age that an Ayr United manager would have no input in team selection. That duty used to be undertaken by the directors at their Monday evening board meeting. The names of the chosen eleven then got passed on to the newspapers with the consequence that people would know the team selection a day or more before the match. No due allowance was made for the experience of the incumbent. When Jimmy Hay was the manager he could reflect on a playing career in which he had captained Scotland, Celtic and Newcastle United. The suited businessmen who made up the directorate still saw fit to tell him his team line-up. There was no intent to undermine the role of the manager. It was simply the protocol of the time. Those Ayr United bosses of long ago did not even have autonomy in the matter of tactics. The game plan was likely to be drawn up at the behest of the more experienced players or less experienced players who happened to have an extrovert nature. In being absolved of responsibilities which 21st century bosses would take for granted, you may well be wondering just what the earliest predecessors did to earn their salary. The answer is that they had a heavier onus on clerical duties. That is why the designation secretary-manager was commonplace.

When a team is going through a halcyon period the manager is revered by the supporters and in times of struggle he is vilified. It was not always so. There was a time when varying fortunes at Somerset Park saw praise or criticism directed at the board. Little or no correlation existed between results and the public mood towards the manager.

The purpose of this book is to study this managerial evolution at Somerset Park and to gain an insight into those men who have occupied the metaphorical hot seat. Did you know that an Ayr United legend was the first Briton to be a football manager in Argentina? In the off chance that you knew that, did you also know that he wasn't the only Ayr United manager to have been contracted to a South American club? Which former Ayr United manager gave Gareth Bale and Theo Walcott their first team debuts? There are quirky facts aplenty in the pages ahead.

Lee Massey – the original Ayr United goalkeeper. In the inaugural 1910/11 season he played in all but one match. This image affords a glimpse of Somerset Park's tarmacadam cycle track.

Harry Murray

May 1910 – May 1914

In the introduction you will have read about the typical profile of the earliest Ayr United managers. Their role tended towards the clerical while team issues were conducted at arm's length. Harry Murray's duties were entirely administrative. The conclusion may therefore be drawn that he was a secretary rather than a manager. It would be a correct conclusion. Yet in the club's pioneering years he was the nearest Ayr United had to a manager. His real name was Henry but he was never called this. Even club communications bore the name Harry.

His job was rendered complex by the intricacy of the amalgamation process. As far back as the summer of 1893 people in the town were talking about a merger between Parkhouse and Ayr FC. In subsequent years the notion became less speculative but the major obstacle was a mutual hatred. Intentional fixture clashing and the spreading of false rumours were typical of the dirty tricks used to undermine each other but in 1904 the plotting hit its lowest level yet. At the end of season 1903/04 Parkhouse finished at the foot of the Second Division and had then to apply for re-election. Parkhouse sent a circular to the voting clubs in the hope of soliciting support. Ayr FC went further than voting against Parkhouse. They sent out a circular in which reasons were outlined not to accord support to their fellow townsmen. It was signed by Harry Murray. Parkhouse temporarily lost their place in the league and the vacancy was filled by Aberdeen. The wounds

Kyle Photo Company, Ayr

AYR UNITED FOOTBALL CLUB.

Back Row—A. Morrison, W. Forsyth (wine mostor), A. Tickle, L. Massie, J. M'Lauchlan, H. M'Kenzi, W. Black, A. Aitken (trainer)

Front Row—J. L. Goodwin, S. Graham, C. Howe, C. Phillips, A. Campbell

This is the earliest surviving Ayr United team group photo. It was taken on 10th September, 1910. This was precisely three weeks after the club had played its first competitive match.

had healed a little by 1909 in which year amalgamation terms were drawn up by the respective boards. Procrastination by Ayr FC caused the proposals to be aborted.

One year later the talks were rekindled under the mistaken impression that an amalgamated club would be voted straight into the First Division. After meetings and counter meetings Ayr United FC got founded on the Monday evening of 9th May, 1910, and, despite the compelling case put together by Harry Murray, life began in the Second Division.

Two boards, two grounds, two sets of shareholders – his secretarial role in making the amalgamation work was gruelling. In suggesting he was outstanding at his job it is not intended to be patronising. He had a flair for administration and credentials which included a Bachelor of Arts. Mr Murray stayed locally at 1 Seaforth Crescent (just off Prestwick Road) and worked as a clerk in the commissary department of the County Buildings. With due allowance for his sterling work for Ayr United it is regretful that he could not have been defined as a manager in the real sense. If it was permitted to be more elastic with the definition he would have been one of the most successful bosses in our history. In the inaugural 1910/11 season the club finished as runners-up in the Second Division. Season 1911/12 succeeded in attaining the Second Division championship. That league campaign began with nine straight wins and this remains a club record at the start of a season. The expression 'Fortress Somerset' might also have been made for this period of history. On 26th November, 1910, Abercorn won 4-3 at Ayr. Ayr United's next home league defeat did not occur until 17th August, 1912, Abercorn again being the opposition. In 1912/13 the title was retained. Then, on the Monday evening of 2nd June, 1913, the club got voted into the First Division.

After relinquishing his post in 1914 Mr Murray continued to be an Ayr United supporter while fulfilling his clerical duties for the council during the week. His cosy existence was soon to be shattered. Shortly after the outbreak of the Great War

Second Division champions 1911/12.

he enlisted in the newly formed Collingwood Battalion of the Royal Naval Division. He was posted to "somewhere in England" and when his clerical qualifications became known he was drafted into the paymaster's department. It was a temporary position. The war situation was crying out for manpower and on the Monday night of 10th May, 1915, he sailed for the Dardanelles. The *Ayrshire Post* dated 24th September, 1915, stated: "In a list of Scottish wounded soldiers and sailors admitted to hospital in Malta on September 7th, 9th and 10th, there appears the name of Henry G. Murray, Anson Battalion, formerly of the Collingwood Battalion of the Royal Naval Division, but no official intimation has been received and the nature and extent of his injuries is not known." He was shipped home for recuperation and he was fit enough to join the Ayr United party for a league fixture at Airdrie on 13th November. A 3-1 defeat was symptomatic of his year to date.

Herbert Dainty

May 1914 – April 1915

Not only was Herbert Dainty the first Ayr United manager in a more conventional sense, he was also our first player-manager. Since then the player-manager label has applied only to George Burley, Simon Stainrod, Gordon Dalziel and Mark Roberts (excepting Brian Reid's term of interim managership in a team of three). The board convened at Somerset Park on the Wednesday evening of 6th May, 1914, and Dainty's appointment was confirmed. He had been a regular at centre-half since making his Ayr United debut in a 3-2 league win at home to Falkirk on 1st November, 1913. His lack of height was more than compensated for by his aggressive tackling.

He was born on 6th February, 1879, in the Northamptonshire village of Geddington. His football career began at nearby Kettering Town and he went on to play for Leicester Fosse, New Brighton Tower, Leicester Fosse again, Northampton Town, Notts County, Southampton, Dundee and Bradford Park Avenue. He then came to Ayr. His biggest achievement in football was playing in Dundee's Scottish Cup winning team of 1910.

Herbert Dainty's one season in charge was successful in the face of struggle. It was a struggle shared by all clubs and the wider public. The Great War was declared on Tuesday, 4th August, 1914, and doubt was cast as to whether the Scottish football season would proceed on Saturday, 15th August. In "almost tropical heat" Partick Thistle were beaten 4-0 at Ayr.

With Dainty playing at centre-half Celtic (1-0) and Rangers (2-0) were beaten on consecutive October Saturdays. This propelled the club into second place in the First Division and it drew forth the following comment from the *Ayrshire Post*: "It is not often that on consecutive Saturdays two such prominent teams as Celtic and Rangers have the same journey to make and the same team to face; but that has occurred in Ayr United's fixtures with the two afore mentioned Glasgow combinations. The story is an old one of the Celtic visit: they came, saw and fell. On Saturday last it was the Rangers' turn to lay siege to the Ayr United forces in their stronghold at Somerset Park; and, as the old country woman said in regard to the news of the battle in the Boer War about which she had known nothing, 'they got a fine day for it.'"

Dainty's tenure was aggravated by players and supporters joining the colours while those engaged in vital war work were subjected to long and erratic shifts which had no cognisance of Saturday afternoons. The abnormal conditions which struck at the finances of the club were inconsistent with results and the league season concluded with Ayr United in fifth place.

By late March 1915 there was speculation that Herbert Dainty would be joining Raith Rovers. There was substance to it because he had business interests in Dundee. Co-incidentally, just after the story broke, he played his last match for Ayr United against Raith Rovers. That was in a scoreless draw. He therefore did not play in the three remaining league fixtures but his managerial position was intact until two days before the last one.

There was a dilemma. He ideally required a move to one of the Dundee clubs. Dundee appeared the logical option since he would have remained in the First Division and he was remembered as a member of their Scottish Cup winning team. Yet the *Ayr Advertiser* reported that: "Dainty will never again don a dark blue shirt."

The same piece explained: "There is no probability of him going to his old club due to a vendetta with the Dens Park crowd." Dundee Hibs (renamed Dundee United in 1923) were keen to sign him but this railed against his desire to play at the top level. He joined them anyway and his career continued in the Eastern League.

Lawrence Gemson

April 1915 – April 1918

Lawrence Gemson was born in Preston in 1873 and herein we have a clue as to what kindled his interest in football. In season 1888/89 Preston North End were the inaugural winners of the Football League and the first winners of a league and FA Cup double. In 1889/90 the championship was retained.

His father George was a publican and by 1891 the family had moved to Glasgow. At the age of twenty-one Mr Gemson moved to Hammersmith to undertake teacher training and he returned to Glasgow where he began teaching at St.Mary's Catholic School.

That was where he got to know the brothers Tom and Willie Maley who had played in Celtic's first ever team. His friendship with the Maleys would eventually work to Ayr United's benefit. Mr Gemson moved to Ayr to undertake the role of headmaster of St.Margaret's commencing on 9th October, 1899. He remained in the job until retiring in 1933.

In 1911 he was appointed to the Ayr United board and with Herbert Dainty's departure east he took on the more onerous position of secretary-manager. When his daily school duties were over he habitually went to Somerset Park to conduct his football business. This was most convenient to his home in Somerset Road.

In season 1915/16 the club finished fourth in the First Division table. It remains a club record for the highest league placing. That this happened under Mr Gemson's charge was inconsistent with his lack of experience in professional football. Being chairman of the Ayr Schools Football Association between 1910 and 1914 was far removed from the position into which he had been thrust. Yet he was intelligent, highly organised, devoted and had good contacts. His greatest strength (or biggest weakness!) was that he was a workaholic. At the same time he was a Fellow of the Educational Institute of Scotland, president of the West of Scotland Catholic Teachers Association, a director of Ayr County hospital, a headmaster and secretary-manager of Ayr United.

Season 1916/17 saw the club slip to twelfth in the First Division and in 1917/18 there was the dubious attainment of picking up the wooden spoon. Local newspapers reporting on that season's final league game also made mention of his retirement as secretary-manager and director.

The reason given was inevitable. It was down to ill-health caused by pressure of work. In 1917/18 the demands of the war created a high turnover of players. Only once was it possible to field the same team on two consecutive Saturdays. Forty-four players were used in competitive action, a figure unsurpassed at Ayr United until 1995/96 when the number was forty-five. The club record turnover was established at forty-six in 1997/98.

In 1922 Mr Gemson was reinstated to the Ayr United board and he became chairman in 1923. He died at the age of seventy-six on 30th January, 1950. His passing took place in his Somerset Road home. Anne and Alice, his daughters, continued to renew their season tickets until passing away respectively in 1975 and 1978.

John Cameron

August 1918 – July 1919

Of all the Ayr United managers no one has stepped into the job with greater credentials than John Cameron. Yet this does not rest with the fact that he had what remains the worst start of any manager at the club. He failed to win any of his first eight games in charge (one draw and seven defeats). These were all league fixtures played between 17th August and 5th October, 1918. The sequence was broken with a 3-2 win away to Hearts on 12th October. In suggesting that there were extenuating circumstances the surface of his story is barely scratched.

Mr Gemson's resignation prompted the secretary-manager's vacancy to be advertised in the newspapers. John Cameron's application would have startled the Ayr United board had they not already been familiar with his fame.

He was raised locally in Wallacetown where his father was a grocer. As a footballer he was conspicuous as an inside-forward with Elmbank and he took a step up by signing for Parkhouse. Then he joined Queen's Park in the summer of 1895. On 28th March, 1896, he was one of four Queen's Park players in the Scotland team which drew 3-3 with Ireland in Belfast. A further move took him to Everton but this was solely on account of his employment with Cunard.

In the autumn of 1898 he was transferred to Tottenham Hotspur and he was their top scorer in his first season there. In 1899 he was appointed as their secretary-manager but continued playing. 1899 also marked the move to White Hart Lane so that made him the first occupant of the manager's office there. Another first was that Spurs first played in white shirts and

John Cameron.

navy shorts under his charge. He won the Southern League with them in 1899/00 and the FA Cup in 1901 at which time the club still had non-league status. As a player and secretary-manager his contribution was immense. In 1908 Spurs got admitted to the Second Division of the Football League but in the same year he returned to Ayr to live in Church Street. At this time he could reflect on being the first ever secretary of the Players' Union.

His acceptance of a coaching assignment in Dresden was ill-timed. He was trapped in Germany upon the declaration of war and was rounded up along with a vast number of British citizens. John Cameron was interned alongside more than 5,000 others at Ruhleben Racecourse on the outskirts of Berlin. What were known as barracks were, in truth, crudely improvised stables. He helped to organise football leagues within the camp and he co-authored a camp football handbook which indicated that there were 453 players within the barbed wire. Most were amateur. Others were professional. The greatest of them all was Steve Bloomer who had been coaching in Berlin at the outbreak of the war. He was the most prolific scorer in England prior to Dixie Dean. There were two leagues comprising fourteen and thirteen teams and the 'barrack' team containing Bloomer was predictably dominant.

In January 1918 Cameron's name appeared on a list of those to be repatriated. Within that month he was back in his home town but he had not fully recovered from the effects of his lengthy captivity. The Ayr United managerial vacancy came at a seemingly convenient time since it afforded him several months of recuperation. Finishing sixth in the First Division table of 1918/19 was an indication that he acquitted himself well. Fifth place was denied by Motherwell having a better goal average. He signed two future Scotland players for the club. Those were Jimmy Hogg from Vale of Clyde and Phil McCloy from Parkhead Juniors.

His career in shipping was resumed and that was why he moved to Leith. At the time of his death in April 1935 his home address was in Easter Road, in close proximity to Hibs' ground.

James MacDonald

August 1919 – Close season 1923

James MacDonald managed Kilmarnock from 1910 until 1919 prior to taking on a similar role at Somerset Park. On his return to Rugby Park with Ayr United on 3rd January, 1920, he was presented with "a handsome timepiece" from the Kilmarnock players.

He quickly established himself as a grafter by setting out to enhance a squad of players which was already quite strong. His job was barely underway when he signed Jock Smith from Neilston Victoria. Smith was a Beith farmer who would go on to play at full-back for Scotland while still attached to Ayr United. Initially he was utilised as a winger at Ayr. The signing-on fee was £10.

After a 1-1 draw at Motherwell on 11th October, 1919, Mr MacDonald had no thoughts about heading home with the Ayr United party. Instead he headed for Larkhall to sign Willie Gibson, a wing-half with St.Anthony's. Willie was one of three footballing brothers and he would go on to win the FA Cup with Newcastle United in 1924 and the Football League title with that club in 1926/27. Sibling Neil would eventually have eleven seasons at Clyde and Jimmy would complete a career spanning Partick Thistle and Aston Villa with the further distinction of being one of the Wembley Wizards of 1928. Their father Neilly had served Rangers and Scotland.

Three weeks prior to the Gibson signing Kilmarnock had been beaten 5-0 at Ayr. Kilmarnock would go on to win that

Ayr United F.C. 1920-21.

season's Scottish Cup by beating Albion Rovers in the final. In the midweek prior to the Kilmarnock rout Albion Rovers were beaten 4-0 at Ayr.

In a 1-1 draw at home to Celtic on 15th November, 1919, the Ayr United forward line contained four present or future Scotland players (Johnny Crosbie, Jimmy Richardson, Neil McBain and Jock Smith). The fifth forward, Billy Middleton, was English. Full-back Phil McCloy and half-back Jimmy Hogg took the total to six.

The post war attendance boom was assisted not only by the pleasing composition of the Ayr United team. War work had been phased out and the demands of manpower by the military was now consigned to history. James MacDonald became the manager at a time when the club was regaining prosperity. In January 1920 it was announced that the board had agreed to buy Somerset Park from W.G. Walker's. Archibald Leitch, the eminent planner of football grounds, was called in, and plans were agreed to extensively renovate the stadium. It took until 1924 for the work to be completed.

In finishing tenth in the 22-club First Division in 1919/20 it was a modest reflection of Ayr United's progress. Yet this was as good as it would get under Mr MacDonald. Fourteenth out of twenty-two was achieved in the next two seasons and tenth place was regained in his final season, 1922/23. That final season in charge was notable not only for the full-back pairing of Smith and McCloy but also the legendary half-back line of Hogg, McLeod and Gibson. It was notable too for eliminating Rangers from the Scottish Cup in front of a then Somerset Park attendance record of 15,853. The 2-0 result was harrowing for the visitors because they were chasing a league and Scottish Cup double to enhance their Golden Jubilee.

There is no documentary evidence to indicate Mr MacDonald's reasons for quitting after the conclusion of that season but it is known to have been harmonious. On the Tuesday evening of 11th December, 1923, a presentation was made to him in Ayr's Market Inn.

Jimmy Richardson

July 1923 – June 1924

Jimmy Richardson's first involvement with Ayr United dates back to March 1914 when he was transferred from Sunderland as a centre-forward. His previous clubs were Kirkintilloch Rob Roy, then Third Lanark, whence he departed for Wearside in 1910. In season 1912/13 Sunderland won the Football League title and lost 1-0 to Aston Villa in the FA Cup final. He was a regular and in the cup final he played in front of a crowd exceeding 120,000 at Crystal Palace.

The move to Ayr seemed inexplicable for a player who was still at his peak. Inexplicable, that is, until the author's conversation with Richardson's grandson who said that his granny (Richardson's wife) could not settle in Sunderland.

Jimmy Richardson is Ayr United's third highest scorer of league goals despite missing more than two seasons through active service in France. He totalled 109 in 159 First Division fixtures, ultimately signing for Millwall in the summer of 1921. His return as manager two years afterwards was understandably popular.

On the Saturday evening of 4th August, 1923, he travelled to Glasgow to sign Billy Brae, an inside-forward with Petershill. Between then and the end of season 1934/35 Brae made 327 league appearances in which he scored 104 goals for Ayr United. It was an inspired first signing. He was willing to cast the net further afield. On 15th December, 1923, Dundee were beaten 2-0 at Ayr while Mr Richardson and two directors were spying on an inside-forward at Cardiff.

Jimmy Richardson.

On 5th January, 1924, Rangers were beaten 2-1 at Somerset Park but to understand the magnitude of victory you require to know that this was their 23rd league fixture of the season and their first defeat.

Such form was replicated in the cup. In 1973 Ally MacLeod became the first Ayr United manager to reach the semi-finals of the Scottish Cup. Had justice prevailed that honour would have been accorded to Jimmy Richardson in 1924. Albion Rovers (3-1) and Kilmarnock (1-0) were beaten at Ayr in the first and second rounds respectively, the latter tie creating a ground record crowd (for then) of 16,721. Clydebank (3-2) were then beaten at Yoker to put the team into the quarter-finals.

At Airdrie, with it tied at 1-1, there was a highly controversial development in the closing seconds. A John McLean shot went wide and, although the ball had crossed the byeline, goalkeeper Jock Ewart returned the ball to open play by kicking it from hand. Referee Humphrey allowed the game to continue. John McLean regained possession then crossed for John Anderson to lash the ball beyond the stricken Ewart.

At this point the Airdrie directors were seen to vacate their seats to make their way to the boardroom. Then, while the Ayr players stood awaiting the recentre, a posse of Airdrie players surrounded the referee in protest at something that wasn't obvious. Referee Humphrey, in spineless fashion, then consulted both linesmen before disallowing it. The reason could only be speculated upon.

It is true that the ball had been kicked from hand when a goalkick should have been taken but play had been allowed to continue besides which this had been to Airdrie's advantage. Another theory was that John McLean had wrongly been adjudged to have been offside. Even into the 1980s it was possible to find old Ayr United supporters who were passionate about the injustice of 1924. A further draw at Ayr preceded a third draw at Ibrox. One day later the teams met again at Ibrox and Hughie Gallacher scored the only goal of the match.

Airdrie went on to win the Scottish Cup.

On the evening of 2nd April, 1924, Ayr United beat Falkirk 2-0. For decades to come this game had a clear recollection for supporters who attended this match. It was a memory of director Lawrence Gemson striding onto the field at half-time to tell full-backs Jock Smith and Phil McCloy that they had been chosen to play for Scotland against England in Wembley's first international match. Both acquitted themselves well in a 1-1 draw.

Fourteenth place out of twenty was the outcome in a chequered season. This could have been construed as a platform on which to build for the following season. Then the *Ayrshire Post* of 13th June, 1924, stated: "Early in the week an announcement was made that Jimmy Richardson had been appointed as manager of Cowdenbeath. It was a surprise to many." The interpretation as a surprise would have been on account of the fact that it was a tough assignment since Cowdenbeath were newly promoted. 1924/25 was to see Cowdenbeath achieve the highest league position in their history. A fifth-placed finish was just two points behind Celtic and they also beat Ayr United home and away.

On 10th March, 1951, Richardson was a spectator at the Ayr United versus Motherwell tie in the quarter-finals of the Scottish Cup. On 31st August that year he died in Glasgow.

Jimmy Hay

June 1924 – January 1926

The newspapers reporting the departure of Jimmy Richardson also reported the appointment of Jimmy Hay (nicknamed Dun) who was quitting the manager's job with Clydebank. There was little time for contemplation and nor should there have been. Managerial experience, a playing career in which he captained Scotland, Celtic and Newcastle United and knowledge of the local area; in a later age such an appointment would have been colloquially described as a shoe-in. Surely with a man of such calibre it was now time to dispense with tradition and allow the manager to pick the team. There was never a hope that this would happen. This trait would have been forgivable had it been successful but when Ayr United lost 4-0 at Cowdenbeath on 20th December, 1924, the *Ayrshire Post* reported criticism of the directors for team selection, most notably for playing Peerie Cunningham out of position.

Jimmy Hay was born at Woodside, a now defunct community near Annbank, on 9th February, 1881. On 11th January, 1902, Ayr FC drew 0-0 at home to Dundee in a Scottish Cup first round tie. The Ayr inside-left suffered an injury and it was known that he would not be fit in time for the replay on the following Saturday. On the Sunday some committee members set out to walk to Jimmy Hay's Annbank home. They had to trudge through six inches of snow on the six-mile trek. Hay had been in dispute with the Annbank club with whom he had been registered so he agreed to sign for Ayr FC.

During the replayed tie at Dundee he was "timid and uncertain" at inside-left. He was moved to left-half when Tom Allan went off injured and the *Ayr Observer* report noted: "He will certainly be a catch for Ayr in that position."

On 7th March, 1903, he played his last competitive game for Ayr FC (there was a friendly against Annbank a week later). The result was a 2-0 win at home to Falkirk. (My grandfather was in the Falkirk team). On Thursday, 19th March, he signed for Celtic. On 7th February, 1903, he had been left out of the team for an away match against St.Bernard's, because it seemed that he was on the verge of signing for Manchester United, in their first season after changing their name from Newton Heath. The St.Bernard's match was abandoned for bad light; the transfer was abandoned, too, because Manchester United baulked at the price.

He won the Scottish Cup with Celtic in 1904, 1907, 1908 and 1911 during which time he attained the captaincy and he played for them when they won six consecutive league titles (1904/05 - 1909/10). In three of his eleven Scotland appearances he was captain. In the summer of 1911 he moved to Newcastle United.

He left Newcastle United at the end of season 1914/15. On 25th July, 1915, he started working as a miner at Drumley Colliery in his native locality and in December that year he began to play for Ayr United. Because he had been a professional footballer prior to July 1915 he was not immune from military conscription. In March 1918 he was called up by the Royal Artillery. Due to being stationed in the area he played for Ayr United in an away match versus Hibs on 20th April, 1918. For the same reason he also guested for Hearts late in season 1917/18.

Hay did not reappear for Ayr United but he was reacquainted as manager in June 1924. The concluding league fixture of season 1924/25 was against Rangers at Ibrox. A draw was needed to escape relegation. While trailing to a 12th minute goal from Billy McCandless, Jimmy McLeod got in a header which missed the goal by a foot. This happened near the end.

The bottom three, in order, were Motherwell, Ayr United and Third Lanark. Each had thirty points but Ayr and Third Lanark were condemned on goal average.

It would take three attempts to regain First Division status and when it did happen Jimmy Hay was not there to witness it. On 27th January, 1926, at a meeting of the Council of the Scottish Football Association, a unanimous decision was made to give him a *sine die* suspension (lifted in 1928).

The trouble dated back to the Third Lanark versus Ayr United fixture on 28th March, 1925. In connection with that match, he had accused club director Tom Steen of attempting to bribe Tom Dougray, the referee. He alleged that Steen arranged for fellow director Alex Stirling to offer Dougray £5 or £10 to ensure an Ayr United win. Stirling would have been a useful intermediary since he was friendly with Dougray. The severity of the accusation was escalated by Steen's position as treasurer of the Scottish Football Association, his tenure being unbroken since 1907. Yet Jimmy Hay's ban was not in punishment for the accusation. It was for his refusal to tender a written apology to Steen. The conclusion that the accusation had no foundation was in direct contradiction to Jimmy Hay's assertion that he was "willing to swear on oath".

His last years were spent working as an insurance agent. On the Thursday morning of 4th April, 1940, he died at his home at 42 Marchfield Road, Ayr, and he was buried at Ayr Cemetery. There were wreaths from Ayr United and Celtic.

Archie Buchanan

January 1926 – September 1931

Mr Buchanan was born on 28th January, 1900; his twenty-sixth birthday occurred one day after Jimmy Hay's ban became effective. His appointment, therefore, began on or just after that birthday and this makes him Ayr United's youngest manager of all time.

On 24th April, 1991, I had the privilege of interviewing him at his home at 43 Oswald Road in Ayr. He had been living there since June 1930, just three months after the death of the previous occupant, who happened to be Sam Aitken, formerly a player with Ayr FC, Middlesbrough, Raith Rovers and Ayr United.

Although aged ninety-one Mr Buchanan could recall certain aspects of life at Ayr United in impressive detail but he was extremely cautious in avoiding issues that were remotely controversial. For example when questioned about the Steen versus Hay issue he said that there were things he could say but he preferred not to. He emphasised that he did not wish to say anything detrimental against anyone. On the subject of Tom Steen he would not be drawn. They must have known each other well quite apart from working together at Ayr United. Mr Steen was the session clerk at the Auld Kirk when Mr Buchanan was an elder there.

Mr Buchanan had no responsibility for engaging players but he was involved with the clerical work pertaining to registrations and transfers. In effect he was running the club

Ayr United FC : 18th August, 1928.

on a full-time basis. When Jimmy Smith was sold to Liverpool in September 1929 he offered Mr Buchanan £5. The money was refused but Smith would not take no for an answer. He bought a clock with the money and all these years later in 1991 he showed me that timepiece. It was still working and had never had to be repaired although it had undergone occasional maintenance.

His father had been on the original Ayr United board and the board of Ayr FC prior to that. At an even earlier phase he had been a committee member of Ayr FC. Young Buchanan was called up by the Highland Light Infantry at the age of eighteen but was most fortunate that the armistice prevented him from active service in France. He entered the Civil Service and worked in the Ayr Labour Exchange prior to making the transformation to employment at Somerset Park. He could clearly recall the 7 p.m. board meetings on a Monday and he spoke about his fellow directors, especially Alec Moffat, Douglas Bowie and Lawrence Gemson. In fact he said that he sometimes called (outside school hours) at Mr Gemson's nearby house for advice. His memory also drifted back to the tarmacadam cycle track at Somerset Park and the sports' meetings staged at the ground. Danny Tolland was one of Ayr United's most skilful players of all time and when his name cropped up Mr Buchanan commented that he had an eye for the ladies.

I asked him about the famous John Thomson playing for Ayr United reserves in December 1926. He said: "We got a boy from Celtic and he lost six goals against a team in the south that went defunct." This was a clear reference to one of Thomson's two appearances for Ayr United reserves, this one being away to the Annan-based Solway Star, albeit that he conceded four goals in that match rather than six. He said, too, that Ayr United could borrow players from Celtic at any time (this was on account of the friendship between Lawrence Gemson and Celtic manager Willie Maley).

Alec Moffat - distinguishable by being the tallest in the back row - with Irvine Meadow in 1898.

Mr Buchanan had a question for me. He asked how much it cost to get into Somerset Park nowadays (nowadays being April 1991) and he seemed taken aback when I told him that it cost £3.50 to stand on the terracing.

Memories of the Scandinavian tour in 1928 were hazy but he did remember the Ayr United party being greeted by a Scottish host when disembarking at Oslo. He could not remember the name but, from the notes on my lap, I was able to tell him that it was Donald Coleman, a former Aberdeen, Dumbarton and Scotland full-back who was then coaching in Norway.

The return to top flight football in 1928 came in spectacular fashion, the Second Division title being won in a free scoring season in which Jimmy Smith scored a record breaking sixty-six league goals. There was no threat of relegation until the concluding match of season 1930/31 when a point was needed in the final match to escape the drop. Compounding the unease was that this match was at home to Kilmarnock. Happily Danny Tolland scored the only goal. It was a goal that caused the supporters to "yell themselves hoarse". In September 1931 Mr Buchanan stepped down.

He died on 27th January, 1994, the day before what would have been his 94th birthday.

Alex Gibson

September 1931 – January 1935

Alex Gibson was appointed on the Thursday evening of
24th September, 1931. He had been a longstanding director
of Kilmarnock, ascending to the role of chairman; he even
became their manager.

Gibson was appointed as the manager of Preston North
End. He was in charge at Deepdale from season 1927/28 until
the end of 1930/31 when there was dissatisfaction at finishing
seventh in the Second Division. It can be fairly assumed that
the dissatisfaction was compounded when they finished
thirteenth in the Second Division table of 1931/32. Interestingly
Manchester United beat them for twelfth place on goal average.

Alex James is one of Scottish football's greatest legends. In
later years Alex Gibson was credited as being the manager who
signed him for Preston North End from Raith Rovers. This
was a contradiction of the *Stranraer Centenary History* (1970)
which stated that James Lawrence was the manager who took
him to Preston. Your writer put this to a Preston historian who
said that the manager in question was neither of them. It was
Frank Richards.

Beyond argument is the fact that Alex Gibson sold him to
Arsenal. Before departing the subject of Alex James you can
be told that his first game in a senior shirt was as a trialist
for Motherwell in a reserve fixture against their Ayr United
counterparts at Beresford Park on 22nd April, 1922.

Ayr United had pulled off a last day relegation escape in
1930/31 and when Mr Gibson arrived on the scene it looked

Ayr United Football Club, Ltd.
1933-34.

DIRECTORS:

A. C. MOFFAT, Esq., *Chairman*.

W. LOCKHART, Esq., *Vice-Chairman.*   A. S. GOVAN, Esq.

D. BOWIE, Esq.   A. A. JACKSON, Esq.

A. WRIGHT, Esq.   J. E. DRINNAN, Esq.

D. MURRAY, Esq.

| A. GIBSON, Manager. | Telephone No.: Ayr 3435. | Registered Office: Somerset Park, Ayr. |

EDITOR'S NOTES.

Our glorious victory over Celtic last week dismisses immediately any suggestion that our position on the League table is a false one, as even allowing for the unusually poor place occupied by the Parkhead team at the present time, it was generally agreed they were more strongly represented on Saturday than since the season opened.

That they were fairly and squarely beaten was also agreed, and let us add willingly admitted by the representatives of the losing side.

As we pointed out last week, during the five seasons which have elapsed since we returned to the First Division, we have not taken a single point from our famous opponents, and this fact makes our win last Saturday all the more welcome.

It was refreshing to see the pluck and keenness with which our young players went into their experienced opponents, and this was obvious from the first sound of the whistle.

Our first goal came rather simply, as it was the result of a misunderstanding between Kennaway and M'Gonagle, but Rodgers made no mistake in the scoring of it.

HALF-TIME SCORE BOARD FOR DECEMBER 2 APPEARS ON PAGE 8.

When O'Donnell equalised, most people thought the game would end this way, but they didn't reckon on the energy and enterprise of our young centre.

If his first—and our second—goal raised enthusiasm what can we say of his other successful effort a minute from the finish—the scene can scarcely be described, and we have no space to attempt it. Suffice to say that the crowd simply went wild with delight, the cheering continuing until the final whistle sounded, and indeed even after the players had disappeared into the dressing rooms.

So now we stand undefeated in our last nine games with every prospect of more success to follow, which fact must be pleasing to every Ayrshire follower of the game.

The success of Kilmarnock at Hampden, we need not remark, is also welcomed—they, too, are doing their bit for the county.

This afternoon Dundee appear at Somerset Park and cannot be taken lightly as they possess a real good side, and from all accounts played splendid football at Paisley last week.

The editorial from the Ayr United versus Dundee programme on 25th November, 1933. The match ended 3-3. Prominent is the reference to beating Celtic 3-1 at Ayr the week before.

as if there would be no such reprieve in the season currently underway. Three draws and eight defeats comprised a miserable start. He was taking over when the club occupied bottom place in the First Division table. Thirty-three league goals had been conceded and the goalkeeper in all but the most recent of those matches (5-1 at Aberdeen) was Bob Hepburn. The fatal injury to John Thomson a fortnight earlier allowed Hepburn to miss the Aberdeen fixture in order to play in goal for Scotland in a 3-1 victory over Ireland at Ibrox.

Even without the power to select the team the required tasks were to stop the rot and plug the defence. His first game was a 2-0 win at home to Dundee United. A draw away to Clyde was followed by home wins over Morton (2-1) and Airdrie (5-1). A relapse then plummeted the team back to the foot, a position still occupied on the last Saturday in November. The last two home league games of the season comprised 5-0 wins (Cowdenbeath and Clyde) and a seventeenth place ensured safety in the 20-club league.

Finishing sixteenth in 1932/33 was trumped by eighth in 1933/34. The relative success of 1933/34 was down to Mr Gibson's best bit of business at Ayr United. In his first senior season since signing from Irvine Meadow, Terry McGibbons had scored thirty-five league goals in addition to being in the Scotland squad for Wembley. In 1983 Terry McGibbons told the author that he got a bus from his native Irvine to Ayr then had to ask for directions to Somerset Park. He then said that Alex Gibson concluded the signing with surprising haste.

On 18th July, 1934, Tommy Robertson, known as The Patna Flyer, signed for Dundee. Even with the loss of an exceptional winger the squad at Mr Gibson's disposal that summer was laced with club legends – Bob Hepburn, Andy McCall, Davy Currie, Billy Brae, Fally Rodger and, of course, the fabulous Terry McGibbons. Bridging September into October four straight league defeats put the club in peril. Twenty goals were conceded in that run culminating in an 8-1 defeat at Falkirk in which Bartram scored six.

The porous defence was in evidence at Dumfries on New Year's Day, 1935, when 11,278 saw Queen of the South take a 7-0 lead by the 63rd minute. It ended 7-1. One day later Kilmarnock were beaten 2-1 at Ayr. Then, on Saturday, 5th January, the defence reverted to their default form in losing 8-0 away to Albion Rovers. The *Glasgow Herald* report patronisingly opined that "the play was by no means one-sided."

Mr Gibson had a firmer grip on reality and at the board meeting on the Monday he announced his resignation. The *Ayr Advertiser* dated 6th March, 1952, reported that he had passed away.

Frank Thompson

January 1935 – June 1940

Frank Thompson first occupied the manager's office at Somerset Park on Monday, 21st January, 1935. His accent betrayed his Irish roots. He was born at Ballynahinch, County Down, on 2nd October, 1888. The more common reports that he was born in 1885 are simply wrong.

He was an outside-left who began his playing career at a club called Black Diamonds. Then he stepped up to Cliftonville. He was in Cliftonville's Irish Cup winning team in 1909 and in their team which lost the final a year later. He signed for Linfield on 23rd November, 1910, but it was a short stay. A move to Bradford City brought him the distinction of playing in their FA Cup winning team of 1911. In 1913 he was transferred to Clyde and, while still a Clyde player, he was appointed as their manager on 27th November, 1922. The Great War had interrupted his career at Clyde and he saw active service in the Dardanelles, Egypt and Salonica. While at Clyde he was still selected for Ireland and he numbered twelve international appearances.

When he became manager of Ayr United the foot of the First Division looked like this.

	P	W	D	L	F	A	Points
Falkirk	28	7	3	18	42	58	17
Ayr United	28	7	3	18	41	90	17
St. Mirren	28	5	4	19	32	59	14

In the final league game of season 1933/34 home team Airdrie needed a point against Ayr United to avoid relegation. In a 1-1 draw they got it. The finale to 1934/35 again threw up

Frank Thompson.

an Airdrie versus Ayr United fixture and this time the visiting team needed a draw to be certain of avoiding relegation. Airdrie did not reciprocate and they won 3-2 with an 88th minute goal. However there was a reprieve. At Broomfield a rumour swept that St. Mirren had beaten Celtic 3-2. Had this been true Ayr United would have fallen through the relegation trapdoor. In truth St. Mirren had lost 2-1 at Celtic Park so they went down with the already doomed Falkirk.

Quite apart from buses and cars there were two packed special trains laid on to take the Ayr support to Airdrie. With a total lack of sympathy for St. Mirren's plight, these trainloads were especially vocal when passing through Paisley on the way home. On the Tuesday afterwards Galston were at Somerset Park for an Ayrshire Cup semi-final. The crowd gave Frank Thompson an ovation when he went onto the field to talk to his players at half-time.

There were no ovations a year later. The team finished at the foot of the league and got relegated with Airdrie. Then came the startling Second Division campaign of 1936/37. In the entire season just one point was dropped at home. This replicated season 1911/12. Mr Thompson was not there to witness the single home point dropped. In March 1937 he spent three weeks in a nursing home in Prestwick and when he got home he was confined to bed. A total of 122 league goals were scored. This remains a club record. Twelve consecutive league wins got registered. This too remains a club record. The championship was won in style.

By the summer of 1939 Ayr United were consolidated in the First Division. A last day relegation escape in April 1938 and the comparative safety of fourteenth (in a 20-club league) one year hence indicated that all was right in the world. Or rather all would have been right in the world had it not been for Hitler. The First Division programme for 1939/40 got expunged after five fixtures whereupon regional leagues were established. Full-time status had to be revoked in favour of training on Tuesday and Thursday nights. There was also the potential difficulty of players getting called up by the military. Eleven of Ayr United's signed players were aged between twenty and twenty-two, thus making them prime candidates for the brown envelope. On 30th May, 1940, the annual general meeting lasted for five minutes. Days later a club statement said: "Ayr United is closed down until further notice."

During the 1945/46 season Frank Thompson went back to Ireland to manage Glentoran. While there he gave the legendary Danny Blanchflower his first break in senior football. Yet he did not settle in his native Ireland.

He died on 4th October, 1950, two days after his 62nd birthday. At this time his home address was 77 Oswald Road, Ayr. He had taken ill while watching a film at Prestwick's Broadway Cinema along with his wife and daughter. On the following day he passed away in hospital.

Bob Ferrier

June 1945 – December 1948

The decision to close the club in 1940 was received badly by the supporters of the time and it also caused internal divisions on the board. More than fifty years later it was possible to find Ayr United supporters willing to testify that closure was a big mistake.

By early 1945 the war in Europe was progressing so satisfactorily that there were murmurings that the club would soon be back in business. On 14th February there was a report that Matt Busby had been named as Ayr United's next manager. Adding credence to the report was the fact that he had just been released by Liverpool. The club officially denied the report. In October that year he took over Manchester United and the eventual Busby Babes had their names written in legend. More positively, the story connecting him to Ayr United at least hinted that the club might soon be operating again.

On 20th June it was correctly reported that Bob Ferrier would be the new Ayr United manager. At this time he was working full-time in Dumbarton and part-time as manager of Airdrie. He also lived in Dumbarton and it was anticipated that it would be mid-July before he would get a proper grip on the Ayr job. Housing was a major problem for the nation as a whole, far less Mr Ferrier. It ultimately took him until August 1946 to get a house in Ayr and he was extremely lucky at that.

Somerset Park was rundown on account of the lack of regular use. It had been used for Junior and representative matches but the weeds had grown high on the terracing. Shabby paintwork further detracted from its pre-war look. It was clear too that the rebuilding on and off the field would be restrained by the financial position. The club was £5,567 in the red.

Mr Ferrier was born in Sheffield but raised in Scotland. He shone as an outside-left with Petershill and he was signed by Motherwell in 1918. His final season as a player there was 1936/37. The longevity was rewarded. He captained Motherwell when they became Scottish champions in 1931/32. There is no doubt that he would have played for Scotland had it not been for his Sheffield birthplace. On retiring as a player he was appointed assistant manager to Sailor Hunter. His next job in football was the manager's position at Airdrie.

Controversially Ayr United got placed in 'B' Division for season 1945/46. No cognisance had been taken of the league positions on the outbreak of war. There were players on the retained list from 1940 but their availability could not be relied upon pending demobilisation. With the league season due to start on 11th August the signing activity was frantic. Yet the process had tentatively begun before Mr Ferrier had been appointed. The first acquisition was Alex Corbett, a 23-year-old goalkeeper with Annbank United. Corbett had been signed as early as March.

Ayr United's first peace-time match since 1939 was a home fixture against Airdrie, a club with which Mr Ferrier was well acquainted. Airdrie had not been the subject of war time closure and they won 3-0 in front of a crowd estimated at 6,500. Within the week centre-half Norrie McNeil was fixed up from Hurlford United and early in September centre-forward Malky Morrison agreed to join from Cambuslang Rangers. Both would acquire the status of legends at Ayr United.

Finishing third in the 14-club league was gratifying when considered against the frenetic organisational effort in the summer of 1945. Less gratifying was a drop of eight places in 1946/47 by which time the team had been bolstered with the inclusion of such fondly remembered players as wing-half Andy Nesbit and outside-left Alec Beattie. It became the old story of the total being less than the sum of its constituent parts. So much individual talent yet eleventh place in 'B' Division was retained in 1947/48.

Stenhousemuir 7 Ayr United 1. This happened on 27th November, 1948, but even before this a rumour had spread that Bob Ferrier would be quitting. On the same weekend as this debacle the rumour was now qualified with the supposed information that he would be off "within three months."

Media requests directed at Somerset Park were met by what the *Ayrshire Post* described as "a wall of silence." A board meeting on the Tuesday still yielded no information. Then, at the end of the week, he handed in his resignation.

Archie Anderson

April 1949 – May 1953

In considering who would replace Bob Ferrier the board could not have been accused of haste. Throughout the locality there was a great deal of speculation on the topic. *The Ayrshire Post* dated 14th January, 1949, went so far as to say: "Will George Paterson, the former Scottish international and Celtic player, be the next manager of Ayr United? At present he is with Brentford. Unconfirmed reports say he has been offered the vacancy."

It transpired that this was true. He had indeed been offered the vacancy following an interview. Then he decided against it and continued to play for Brentford. Later in 1949 he moved into management at Yeovil Town.

In February the board officially denied that they had interviewed either Archie Anderson, the manager of Arbroath, or referee Bobby Calder, the former manager of Dunfermline Athletic and future legendary scout for Aberdeen. Director R.W. Hutchison endorsed the denials by using the description "nonsense". This was inconsistent with Archie Anderson being spotted at Somerset Park on Friday, 25th February and it was grossly inconsistent with him being appointed at a board meeting on 15th March. December 1948 until March 1949 comprised a conspicuously long period for the managerial void to persist. It was a situation aggravated when it was made known that there was uncertainty about how long a period of notice he would have to work with Arbroath.

AYR UNITED FOOTBALL AND ATHLETIC CLUB, LTD.

Colours: White Jerseys and Blue Knickers

SOMERSET PARK
AYR
Tel. 3435

Secretary-Manager
ARCHIBALD ANDERSON

AYR UNITED'S FIXTURES, 1950-51.

League Cup —"B" Division, "A" Section.

		Goals For	Agst.	Pts.
1950.				
Aug. 12—Dumbarton	A	4...	1...	2...
,, 16—Kilmarnock	H			
,, 19—D'fermline Ath.	H			
,, 26—Dumbarton	H			
,, 30—Kilmarnock	A			
Sept. 2—D'fermline Ath.	A			

"B" Division.

Sept. 9—St. Johnstone	A			
,, 16—D'fermline Ath.	H			
,, 23—Kilmarnock	A			
,, 30—Stenhousemuir	H			
Oct. 7—Hamilton Accies.	A			
,, 14—Dumbarton	H			
,, 21—Cowdenbeath	H			
,, 28—Arbroath	A			
Nov. 4—Forfar Ath.	H			
,, 11—Stirling Albion	A			
,, 18—Queen's Park	H			
,, 25—Alloa Ath.	A			
Dec. 2—Dundee United	A			
,, 9—Queen of South	H			
,, 16—Albion Rovers	A			
,, 23—St. Johnstone	H			
,, 30—D'fermline Ath.	A			
1951.				
Jan. 1—Kilmarnock	H			
,, 2—Stenhousemuir	A			
,, 6—Hamilton Accies.	H			
,, 13—Dumbarton	A			
,, 20—Cowdenbeath	A			
,, 27—SCOTTISH CUP—First Round.				
Feb. 3—Arbroath	H			
,, 10—Forfar Ath.	A			
,, 17—Stirling Albion	H			
,, 24—Queen's Park	A			
Mar. 3—Alloa Ath.	H			
,, 10—Dundee United	H			
,, 17—Queen of South	A			
,, 24—Albion Rovers	H			

"C" DIVISION FIXTURES.

League Cup

		Goals For	Agst.	Pts.
1950.				
Aug. 12—Partick Thistle	H	3...	2...	2...
,, 16—Queen's Park	A			
,, 19—Queen of South	A			
,, 26—Partick Thistle	A			
,, 30—Queen's Park	H			
Sept. 2—Queen of South	H			

" C " Division

,, 9—Airdrieonians	H			
,, 13—Rangers	A			
,, 16—St. Mirren	A			
,, 20—Partick Thistle	H			
,, 23—Kilmarnock	H			
,, 27—Morton	A			
,, 30—Third Lanark	H			
Oct. 7—Stranraer	H			
,, 14—Stranraer	A			
,, 21—Queen of South	A			
,, 28—Dumbarton	A			
Nov. 4—Partick Thistle	A			
,, 11—Hamilton Accies.	H			
,, 18—East Stirling	A			
,, 25—Queens Park	H			
Dec. 2—Clyde	A			
,, 9—Kilmarnock	A			
,, 16—Motherwell	H			
,, 23—Airdrieonians	A			
,, 30—St. Mirren	H			
1951.				
Jan. 1—Dumbarton	A			
,, 2—Motherwell	A			
,, 6—Hamilton Accies.	A			
,, 13—Third Lanark	H			
,, 20—Rangers	H			
,, 27—Queen of South	H			
Feb. 3—Queens Park	A			
,, 24—Morton	H			
Mar. 10—Clyde	A			
,, 17—East Stirling	H			

From the Ayr United versus Kilmarnock programme dated 16th August, 1950. Note Archie Anderson's title of secretary-manager. Somewhat quaintly shorts are referred to as knickers in the section denoting colours. The advert for Manfield-Hotspur football boots evokes memories of an age when boots truly were boots.

Mr Anderson was a widower and he planned to live in Ayr. It was also his plan to make weekend visits to his family who were to live with relatives in Blantyre. He had been manager of Blantyre Victoria prior to managing Arbroath whom he took to the Scottish Cup semi-finals in 1947 at which stage they lost 2-0 to Aberdeen at Dundee's Dens Park.

During the last week in April 1949 Ayr United played in a Highland tour by which time he had managed to extricate himself from his employment at Arbroath. It was a punishing intinerary with games played on Saturday (Buckie Thistle), Monday (Inverness Thistle), Wednesday (Stornoway select), Thursday (Elgin City), Friday (Fraserburgh) and the next Saturday (Deveronvale). Every game was won and nineteen goals were scored in the process. The top scorer was 'Waggie' Ross with eight. He was a guest player from, as if you have not guessed, Arbroath.

At first glance season 1949/50 was a failure with a thirteenth place finish in the 16-club 'B' Division. Yet a most impressive statistic had already taken root. On 21st January, 1950, Cowdenbeath won 2-1 at Ayr. It was the club's last home league defeat until 13th September, 1952, when Stenhousemuir won 4-2 at Somerset Park. Between those dates Ayr United were unbeaten in thirty-three consecutive home league games and this remains a club record. The nearest comparison related to an unbeaten home league run between 26th November, 1910, and 17th August, 1912. In the year of writing there are only five seasons in which Ayr United have gone through the entire campaign unbeaten at home in the league: 1911/12 (champions Second Division), 1936/37 (champions Second Division), 1950/51 (third 'B' Division), 1951/52 (third 'B' Division) and 2008/09 (runners-up new style Second Division). Two out of the five with Archie Anderson in charge and the only Ayr United manager to do it consecutively! It was regrettable though that each time the club landed one place short of one of the two promotion places.

Since this photo was in Len Round's scrapbook it is understandable that he is the goalkeeper shown. The action is from the Ayr United versus Motherwell tie in the Scottish Cup quarter-finals on 10th March, 1951. Also visible are Alex Perrie (3) and Andy Nesbit (6). The lone Motherwell attacker is Jim Forrest. There were no health and safety fears then as evidenced by some of the 22,152 crowd being housed on

On the subject of club records Mr Anderson has a further one to his credit. He was the first Ayr United manager to reach a national semi-final. Season 1950/51 opened with Ayr United in a League Cup section with Dumbarton, Kilmarnock and Dunfermline Athletic. In scoring sixteen goals for the loss of five, the six sectional ties yielded five wins and a draw. Winning the section brought about a quarter-final pairing with Dundee United. The first leg was won 3-0 at Ayr in a tie played in almost continuous heavy rain. That was on the Saturday. On the Wednesday the second leg was won 2-1 at Tannadice Park for a tidy 5-1 aggregate. This set up a semi-final against Motherwell at Ibrox on 7th October, 1950.

Telegrams wishing good luck were received from Kilmarnock, Inverness Caledonian and Coylton Juveniles. The one from Kilmarnock was especially gracious considering that they had been eliminated from the competition by Ayr United. A Raith Rovers Supporters' Club also sent a telegram to their former players Ian Crawford and Hugh Goldie. Suitably inspired Goldie and Crawford (twice) scored. The 3-2 lead was fragile and the tie was lost 4-3 through late goals from Johnny Aitkenhead (83) and Jimmy Watson (85).

His feat in taking an Ayr United team to a national semi-final had been without precedent but Mr Anderson came very close to repeating the feat in the same season. For the Scottish Cup quarter-final against Motherwell on 10th March, 1951, a crowd of 22,152 crammed into Somerset Park. With the score at 1-1 a leg-breaking tackle was made by Archie Shaw on Ayr scorer Jimmy Baker. It was so bad that Baker did not play first team football again until January 1952. In the immediate term Ayr United had to complete the tie a man short, referee Davidson reaching the insane conclusion that the challenge did not merit a dismissal. Ian Crawford nevertheless put the team into a half-time lead. Jim Forrest (60) salvaged a replay for Motherwell.

The action reverted to Fir Park on the Wednesday, Motherwell winning 2-1 by a Donald McLeod goal in the final minute of extra time.

Landing just short of a promotion slot in the two seasons prior, expectation was high when 1952/53 was being embarked upon. Mr Anderson used his Blantyre connections to sign Gordon Finnie from Blantyre Victoria. Yet Finnie was not in the team on the evening of 13th August when another club record was set. Ayr United 11 Dumbarton 1 is also a record win in the history of the League Cup competition, although it is shared with Albion Rovers 1 Partick Thistle 11 at Motherwell's Fir Park on 11th August, 1993. The annihilation of Dumbarton created false hope. 1952/53 came to an end with promotion still proving to be elusive.

Mr Anderson himself shared the view that fifth place was unsatisfactory and on the Friday evening of 15th May, 1953, he resigned.

Reuben Bennett

June 1953 – April 1955

2nd June 1953 – the Coronation of Queen Elizabeth II : also on 2nd June 1953 – news reaches Britain that Mount Everest has been conquered : 23rd June – Reuben Bennett is appointed manager of Ayr United. In a momentous month such as June 1953 Mr Bennett's appointment was never going to achieve a blaze of publicity. Yet the march of time would see him associated with fame as a member of the famous 'boot room' at Liverpool.

He was born in Aberdeen on 21st December, 1913, and in his youth he developed into an outstanding goalkeeper. In season 1935/36 he was at Hull City and his next club was Queen of the South, whom he joined in 1936/37. During the war he turned out for Aberdeen, his hometown club. Post war he played for Dundee but he was hampered by a muscle injury in 1948 and stopped playing. In 1950 he signed for Elgin City where he played for one season. Then he returned to Dundee as part of the coaching team.

After negotiating through a League Cup section involving Stenhousemuir, Albion Rovers and Queen's Park, his Ayr United team reached the quarter-finals of the League Cup. This threw up a very stern test for Mr Bennett. Rangers over two legs! On the Saturday afternoon of 12th September, 1953, Rangers won their home leg 4-2. Leg two was in front of an all-ticket Somerset Park crowd on the Wednesday. Of necessity in those pre-floodlight days it was a 5.30 p.m. kick-off. Willie

Fraser drove the ball against the Rangers post in the opening attack. Mike McKenna had better luck in the 10th minute when his terrific drive did find the net. Eleven minutes later it was 2-0 on the night and 4-4 on aggregate. A Joe Hutton drive was handled by Willie Woodburn and the resultant penalty was converted by Willie Fraser. At the opposite end Willie Waddell scored with a penalty after Derek Grierson was brought down. Ten minutes into the second half Willie Paton (future Ayr United) headed in a Sammy Cox free-kick to square it at 2-2 on the night. Joe Hutton's drive put Ayr 3-2 ahead with ten minutes to go. At 6-5 down on aggregate and with two minutes to go Norrie McNeil narrowly missed with a header from a Bobby Cairns free-kick.

Coaching was Reuben Bennett's strength and he appeared to have proven that he could coax big performances from the players at his disposal. Clubs of Rangers' stature would not be met on a weekly basis in 'B' Division. Credence was given to this confidence when the first three league fixtures of the season were won : 4-0 at home to Cowdenbeath, 1-0 at home to Kilmarnock and 4-3 away to Motherwell. Two of these wins were against clubs who were considered to be major contenders for promotion. Rightly so – Motherwell went on to win the league with Kilmarnock promoted as runners-up. The next three league matches were lost : 2-1 at home to Stenhousemuir, 3-1 away to Dumbarton and 4-3 at home to St. Johnstone.

After losing 2-1 at home to Dunfermline Athletic on 14th November, 1953, the *Ayrshire Post* coverage carried some pessimism with a hint of optimism despite a headline containing no ambiguity. **PROMOTION CHANCES DWINDLE**. Accompanying editorial contained a glorious example of the old cliché about the glass being half full or half empty. "The Ayr management will have to rebuild if the team is to gain 'A' Division status." So, in broad terms, the team was deemed to be not good enough but it was implied that promotion could still happen. This sentiment was not shared by the general public. One week later a 4-2 defeat away to Albion Rovers prompted the *Ayrshire Post* football writer to mention that: "At Coatbridge on Saturday there was not one supporters' bus to be seen." The cause of defeat was laid bare in the headline. **DIRECT ACTION DEFEATS ARTISTRY.** Clearly the team was capable of playing good football just so long as the opposition was prepared to stand back and allow it to happen.

On Christmas Day 1953 Reuben Bennett travelled to Stoke. Joe Hutton travelled with him and he accepted Stoke City's terms. Stoke City also had an interest in Bobby Cairns, who put pen to paper for them the next morning while still in Scotland. Cairns then spectated at Ayr United 3 Arbroath 0 in the afternoon. This double transfer was partly compensated by Jacky Robertson making a scoring return on Boxing Day, in what was his first match of the season after suffering from a cartilage problem. The exceptional form of fellow forward Alec Beattie was another cheering aspect when entering 1954. Kilmarnock 0 Ayr United 3 – New Year's Day was even more festive than normal.

It did not take long for 1954 to degenerate. A scoreless draw at home to Dumbarton on 16th January drew the comment that: "This was the worst game seen at Somerset Park this season." In the modern age this comment would have been copied and pasted onto the report of the next home match which ended Ayr United 0 Third Lanark 6. Ally MacLeod was "the tall fairheaded MacLeod" referred to in the Third Lanark team.

Coaching was Reuben Bennett's forte and in the build-up to the following week's Scottish Cup tie at Berwick we can be sure that he was behind the quote issuing from Somerset Park: "The players will be instructed to go all out from start to finish."

On the day of the Third Lanark demise, the injured Norrie McNeil spied on 'C' Division Berwick Rangers in their match against Aberdeen reserves. 'C' Division – this was the same level as Ayr United reserves who played in the south and west division as opposed to Berwick's participation in the north and east division. What was there to fear for an Ayr United team facing a side of a similar calibre to their own reserves? The club's only previous visit to Berwick in the Scottish Cup had yielded a 9-3 win on 19th January, 1929. Berwick Rangers 5 Ayr United 1 was the catastrophic outcome this time. The *Ayrshire Post* rightly held nothing back in expressing condemnation: "After this fiasco the only thing to do is start team building – at once!" The same edition also carried: "The United management know how crestfallen the supporters are and there are talks of a boycott." The boycott materialised. For a 4-2 defeat at home to Alloa Athletic on 3rd April, 1954, the crowd was put at "600". This was in contrast to the estimated Ayr support of 10,000 for the League Cup tie at Ibrox back in September. A ninth place finish was another setback.

The Scottish Cup fiasco of 1954 was replicated in 1955. A 1-1 draw was played out against Inverness Caledonian at Telford Street on 5th February. Even although the replay was on a Wednesday afternoon the attendance figure of 4,217 was considered to be derisory. The result was equally derisory – Ayr United 2 Inverness Caledonian 4 after extra time. Against Highland League opposition this was too much to bear. In later years supporters would recall this as being the end for Reuben Bennett. He persevered for another two months then resigned on the Monday evening of 11th April despite having won his last three league games, one of which was 2-0 at home to Third Lanark. The relevance here is that the earlier meeting at Cathkin Park had finished 9-0 in favour of the Thirds. With just four league games left the timing of his departure was curious.

On 13th September, 1955, Reuben Bennett got his next job in football. It was a coaching role at Motherwell. Then, on 4th December, 1956, he became the manager of Third Lanark. In December 1958 he went to Liverpool as a coach and he remained there until the end of season 1985/86. He died on 14th December, 1989.

So why was this much revered coach of the Shankly era and beyond barely remembered as an Ayr United manager? Well, even in the 1950s an Ayr United manager was still expected to fulfil administrative duties. It is only a theory but he may have been distracted by clerical matters when he only wanted to be a tracksuit manager.

Neil McBain

1. April 1955 – August 1956

Reuben Bennett's links with Ayr United were broken on a Monday and his replacement was named at the end of the week. The new arrival was Neil McBain, the third former Ayr United player to hold the managerial position at the club. Four league games remained to be played. His inauguration was a 3-0 defeat at Alloa and the season petered out into a final league position of eighth.

On 30th May, 1914, Neil McBain played in the Campbeltown Academicals team in the replayed Renfrewshire Cup final against Neilston Victoria at Ayr's Beresford Park. His performance at inside-left was exceptional in this Saturday evening tie. After the match he signed for Ayr United in the nearby Ayrshire and Galloway Hotel.

He was Campbeltown-born on 15th November, 1895, so it was a big commitment for the eighteen-year-old, but the declaration of war in August would have required him to uproot from his native locality anyway. Military service meant that by the time he had been four years at the club his league appearances amounted to a mere seven.

He served with the Argyll and Sutherland Highlanders and the Submarine Service and it is on record that he guested for both Portsmouth and Southampton. Only from October 1918 did he become a regular in the Ayr team even although he was not discharged until March 1919. By the closing weeks of 1919/20 there was the realisation that his best position was

Neil McBain.

as a half-back rather than an inside-forward. In the summer of 1921 he toured Canada with a Scotland squad. There were twenty-five games (all won except for one draw) in twelve weeks. In November 1921 he was sold to Manchester United for £4,600. This was a massive transfer fee in its day - about £700,000 today for the average wage-earner - even comprising what was then a club record purchase for them. In the year of writing their record transfer fee is the £89,000,000 paid for Paul Pogba. In January 1923, by which time Manchester United had been relegated, Neil McBain was sold to Everton. While there he got two Scotland caps to add to the one he got while at Old Trafford. It is a fact that when the legendary Dixie Dean made his Everton first team debut (Arsenal away, 21st March, 1925) his captain was Neil McBain. In the summer of 1926 he was transferred to St. Johnstone where he was appointed captain. Then, in March 1928, he was transferred to Liverpool. In November of that year he went to Watford as a player-manager, eventually becoming manager only, a role he held until the summer of 1937. Season 1937/38 initially saw him as a scout at Luton Town but by March 1938 he had managerial control, his position being ratified in June.

With the intervention of war he became employed as a joiner and he returned to football with a move to Merseyside to manage New Brighton. On 15th March, 1947, former Ayr United goalkeeper Alex Corbett experienced travelling difficulties in connection with New Brighton's match at Hartlepool. At the age of 51 years 4 months Mr McBain deputised in goal thereby giving him the record (still standing) of being the oldest player to have made an appearance in the Football League. On 19th April, 1919, he had made a one-off appearance in goal for Ayr United in a friendly at Kilmarnock. The match at Hartlepool was lost 3-0.

In February 1948 he accepted the post of assistant manager at Leyton Orient and by August he was the manager. His one season as manager at Brisbane Road was followed by a most extraordinary move. In March 1950 he moved to Argentina to take charge of Estudiantes, eventually returning in 1951. He was the first Briton to be a football manager in Argentina. Between September and October 1968 Estudiantes beat Manchester United over two legs to win the World Club championship. Neil McBain was the only man to have had a connection with both clubs.

The concluding weeks of season 1954/55 afforded him the opportunity to assess what was, in effect, Reuben Bennett's team. His first signing was Willie 'Puskas' Hendry, an inside-forward, from Annbank United. Next came Adam Haugh, a wing-half, from Annbank United and Bobby Stevenson, a centre-forward, from Auchinleck Talbot. Next in were Sam McMillan, a teenaged inside-forward, from Irvine Meadow and Peter Price, a centre-forward, who was registered with Gloucester City but had been playing for Darlington owing to a National Service posting in that area.

Acquiring McMillan and Price attracted minimal column inches but this can be attributed to a lack of the gift of prophecy. Peter Price, a native of Mossblown, remains the greatest Ayr United player of all time. His career at the club yielded 213 goals in 251 competitive appearances. Sam McMillan went on to score 127 competitive goals for Ayr United, leaving him with the distinction of having scored more goals for the club then anyone apart from Peter Price. Contract rebel Willie Japp was re-signed after a conversation with chairman Matt Pollock.

There were no outlandish predictions of promotion that summer. Not that they would have been wayward. In finishing runners-up to Queen's Park promotion was achieved with 103 'B' Division goals being scored over the thirty-six fixtures. Peter Price got precisely forty of them. The team of 1955/56 could be recited for years to come: Round, Leckie, Thomson, Traynor, Gallagher, Haugh, Japp, McMillan, Price, Stevenson and Beattie.

From season 1956/57 the leagues were rebranded as the First and Second Divisions rather than Divisions 'A' and 'B'. Such trivia would not have been on Neil McBain's mind during that intemperate summer of 1956. The *Ayrshire Post* dated 3rd August, 1956, carried some chilling news: "Neil McBain has asked the board for a contract. He has been offered good terms to manage Watford and unless the Ayr directors are willing to offer him a contract he threatens to resign and go to Watford."

The threat materialised and he did indeed go to Watford to fill the void created by the sacked Len Goulden. Confirmation of the move came in the week leading up to the opening of the Scottish season. In February 1959 his contract at Watford was terminated.

Jacky Cox

August 1956 – November 1961

In preparation for the challenge of top flight football Neil McBain worked hard in the 1956 close season. Bobby Bell (Falkirk), Guy Lennox (Clyde), Matt Murray (Kilmarnock), Tommy Anderson (Falkirk), Joe McAvinney (Troon Juniors) and Willie Gillies (Bath City) – in recruiting these players Mr McBain could have had no expectation of the Watford vacancy which left Ayr United without a manager desperately close to the new season. The opening League Cup sectional tie was lost 6-1 away to Second Division Dundee United. Disorientation would have been a convenient excuse although we can be sure that the fans were less discerning in their words of criticism. Newspapers reporting a midweek 3-3 draw at home to Third Lanark also carried the news that the new manager would be Jacky Cox. By the time he was installed in the job League Cup qualification was not a prospect but he pulled off a 5-1 win away to Third Lanark. The real challenge was the First Division.

He was a native of Darvel who was playing for his local junior club when spotted by Hamilton Accies. His debut for Hamilton was in the second match of the 1931/32 season. Coincidentally it was a First Division fixture at Ayr (Ayr United 1 Hamilton Accies 3). In season 1934/35 Hamilton Accies finished fourth in the First Division and lost 2-1 to Rangers in the Scottish Cup final. With Jacky Cox at left-half these were glory days for both player and club. This much was apparent to Preston North End who offered him appealing terms.

Jacky Cox.

In August 1939 Jacky Cox and Terry McGibbons joined Ayr United from Preston North End. In the case of McGibbons it was a matter of rejoining since the club had sold him to Preston the summer before. In correspondence with Preston North End historian Ian Rigby, the author got an interesting insight on the deal. Here are Mr Rigby's words, complete with his punctuation: "We bought him (Terry McGibbons) for £1,950 and he went back in a double deal with Jacky Cox for £1000, each player being valued at £500!!!! North End only ever received £500 due to the war and wrote off the balance."

The declaration of war caused the league programme to be expunged after five matches had been played. Full-time contracts were converted to part-time contracts of £2 per week. Jacky Cox combined his football with shipyard work and he saw the season out in the quickly convened Regional League. With Ayr United no longer operational he joined Partick Thistle for season 1940/41. His next clubs were St. Mirren and Stranraer. The *Stranraer Centenary History*, published in 1970, stated: "He was undoubtedly the hardest and most fearless right-half ever played by Stranraer. His name is one that must be recorded in the history of the club".

In those post war years Stranraer existed in the Southern Counties League, then 'C' Division. It was only in 1955/56 that the club got accepted into the proper league status accorded by 'B' Division. By then they had lost their captain Jacky Cox. In December 1953 he became the manager of Hamilton Accies, a role he relinquished when accepting the Ayr job in August 1956.

The task of survival was just too great in 1956/57. On finishing bottom there were nine free transfers and a further three were open to transfer. Winger Alec Beattie, who had excelled on the left wing for Ayr United since 1946, was in a car accident on 7th July, 1957. It happened on a Sunday morning while driving from his home in Parkhead to his work at Hillington. He lay in a coma until passing away on 30th July. Mr Cox, while holidaying in Blackpool, had been getting daily telephone updates on his position. The situation was a tragedy in the real sense. On losing away to Partick Thistle in the last league fixture of 1956/57 the *Ayrshire Post* report had said: "What would Ayr do without the effervescent Beattie?" That question would now be answered.

Scoring ninety-eight goals in thirty-six league fixtures (including forty-six from Peter Price) would have been promotion form had it not been for the number eighty-one in the 'goals against' column. The frustration of fifth place would be banished in the season ahead. In 1958/59 the Second Division championship was not so much won as conquered. Four club records were broken and they still stand. They were: twenty-eight league wins; seven consecutive away league wins; seventeen consecutive league games unbeaten and, most impressively of all, 139 goals were scored comprising 115 in the league, four in the Scottish Cup and twenty in the League Cup.

1959/60 held no particular fears for Mr Cox's team and he was left with the distinction of being the only Ayr United manager to have beaten Rangers and Celtic away in the same season. On 19th September, Rangers were beaten 3-0 and even that result did not fully illustrate Ayr United's superiority. Seven weeks later Celtic were beaten 3-2 at Celtic Park. For a match against Hearts, on 3rd October, so many supporters turned up for the special train that British Railways had to lay on another one. This was in addition to the large number of cars and buses.

If justice had prevailed Jacky Cox would have been the first Ayr United manager to lead the club into a European competition. The Anglo-Franco-Scottish Friendship Cup comprised eight clubs from France, four from England and four from Scotland (excepting those who had qualified for the other European competitions). Based on the league positions at the end of 1959/60 Ayr United (eighth) should have qualified for the forthcoming season. Yet our place had to be conceded to Celtic who had finished one position lower. The issue was Somerset Park having no floodlights. Gallingly we had to accept Celtic, rather than Ayr United, playing Sedan.

Hearts away on 3rd October, 1959

With no European horizons to contemplate at least the prospect of the domestic season had no fears. The confidence was a hoax. Bottom place and relegation was Ayr United's lot by April 1961. This did not square with the fact that Hearts (reigning champions), Rangers (on course for the title) and Dunfermline Athletic (on course to win the Scottish Cup) were all beaten at Ayr.

In conversation Peter Price once told the author that there were times when he did not get on well with Jacky Cox and that his favourite Ayr United manager was "Auld Neilly". Price was dropped for four of the five matches played in October 1960 despite being the club's top scorer to that point of the season. In the summer of 1961 the great man was offered terms involving a £2 cut in wages.

Even with that contractual dispute resolved the season ahead stood to be tempestuous in other ways. A 4-1 defeat at Stranraer on the evening of 27th September was described as "a low ebb" by the *Ayr Advertiser*. A 1-1 draw at Forfar on the Saturday had the same journalist complaining of a lack of punch, cohesion and confidence. On the Tuesday evening of 28th November, Mr Cox resigned.

In December 1962 he became manager of St. Mirren, a position he held until the end of 1964/65. On 23rd October, 1965, he attended an Ayr United versus Raith Rovers match in his capacity of Fulham's chief scout for Scotland.

He passed away in 1990.

Bobby Flavell

1. November 1961 – December 1961

After Jacky Cox's resignation on the Tuesday, Bobby Flavell was named as the new manager on the Thursday. The managerial reign on which he was about to embark would amount to the shortest in the club's history (excepting periods of interim management). Seventeen days! Although not privy to what took place it is a reasonable assumption that the directors were most impressed by Mr Flavell's background in football. His playing career started with his local club Airdrie in season 1937/38. As a centre-forward he later appeared for Hearts, Dundee, Kilmarnock and St. Mirren. As a wartime guest he also played for Arsenal, Brentford, Crystal Palace, and Spurs. His wartime appearance against England was supplemented by two more Scotland appearances post war. In a headline-catching development he quit Hearts in 1950 to go and play for Millionarios, a club based in Bogota, the capital of Colombia. One of his team mates there was future Real Madrid great Alfredo di Stefano.

Here in 1961 he left a coaching job with St. Mirren to tackle the job of restoring Ayr United's rapidly fading glory. On Thursday, 14th December, by which time he had taken charge of two matches, he got a phone call inviting him to a meeting with two St. Mirren directors in an Ayr hotel. He thought that they were looking to open up transfer talks for Alastair McIntyre. On the same day St. Johnstone boss Bobby Brown signed McIntyre for £7,000. In any event St. Mirren were not pursuing an interest in McIntyre. The deputation offered Mr Flavell the job of managing their club.

On the next day he was at Somerset Park and, in a seeming hint at normality, he re-opened negotiations for the transfer of Tommy Henderson from Hearts. Chairman Matt Pollock, knowing of the imminent departure of his manager, began to consider prospective candidates for a replacement. On the Saturday morning there were headlines about Bobby Flavell being on the verge of rejoining St. Mirren. A lesser priority was given to the comparatively minor story that Tommy Henderson had refused to join Ayr United. After a 5-1 win at home to Brechin City, Mr Flavell told the players that he was going back to St. Mirren. This was three games and seventeen days after leaving that same club.

However, as you will read in the pages ahead, he was destined to return. Even with due allowance for the brevity of his tenure it was ironic that Bobby Flavell arrived at Ayr to replace Jacky Cox because eventually Jacky Cox would replace Bobby Flavell as manager of St.Mirren.

Gerry Mays

December 1961 – December 1962

You will have read that Bobby Flavell's initial 17-day stint terminated with him shaking hands with the Ayr United players after a 5-1 win at home to Brechin City on 16th December, 1961. On Sunday, 17th December, a special board meeting was held. At that meeting Gerry Mays was appointed as the new manager. Aged forty he was employed as a coach with Kilmarnock at this time. He said his goodbyes at Kilmarnock on the Monday then took over at Ayr on the Tuesday. If the name was vaguely familiar to some supporters it was because his older brother Jock had signed for Ayr United in October 1936. He came as part of a signing coup in which Frank Thompson went to his old club Clyde to swoop for three players. The other two were Eddie Summers and Albert Smith. Mr Thompson had signed all three for Clyde.

Gerry Mays had been an inside-forward whose playing career spanned Hibs, St. Johnstone, Dunfermline Athletic and Kilmarnock. Coaching seemed a natural progression but management presented an altogether more formidable challenge. His first weekend in the job was a blank Saturday. This was merely down to the nonsensical 19-club set-up in the Second Division, the odd number compelling one club to have no fixture on a weekly basis. Then, on the last Saturday of the year, he eased into management with a 1-1 draw at Montrose. On the Monday (New Year's Day) Morton were slain 4-1 at Somerset Park. Was this a sign of better days to come?

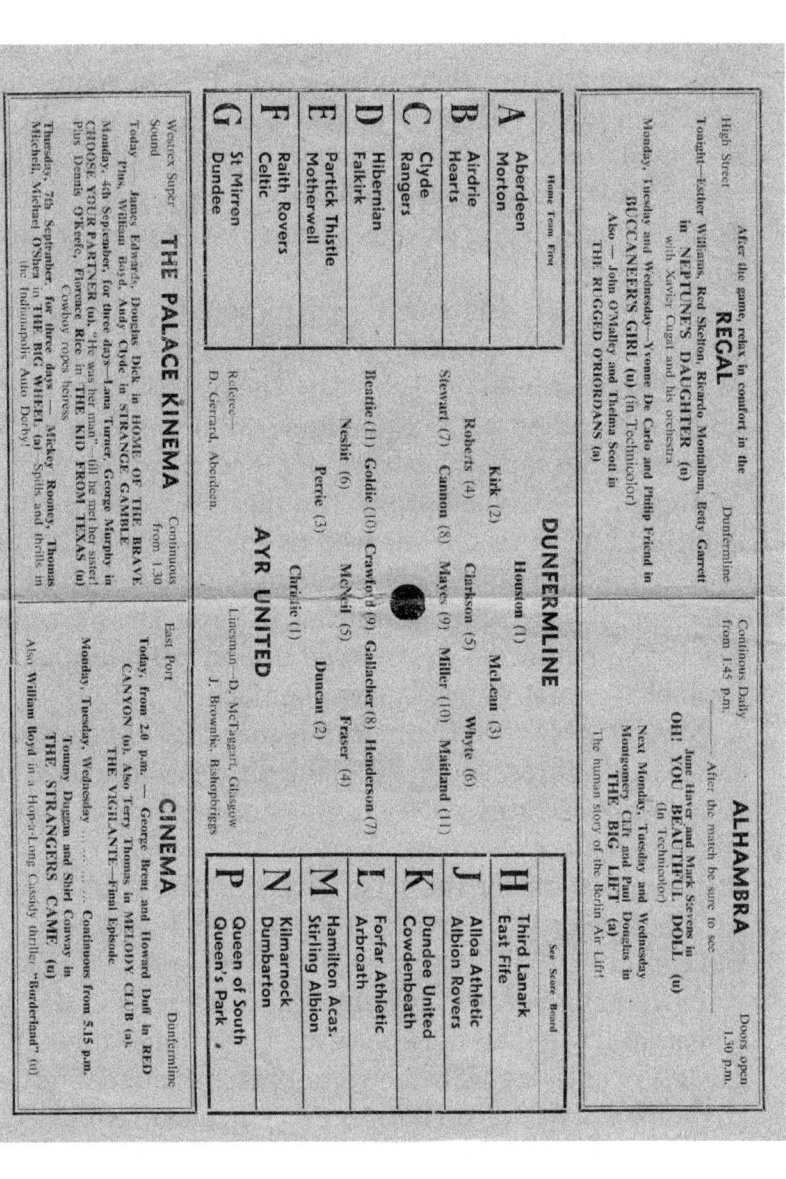

The centrepiece of this Dunfermline Athletic versus Ayr United programme shows Gerry Mays listed at centre-forward for the home team. The programme is dated 2nd September, 1950. His name (Mays/Mayes) was regularly the subject of conflicting spelling.

It wasn't! The next three games were lost, the last of which was a 7-2 defeat at Alloa. Compounding that humiliation was the fact that Alloa played most of the second half with ten men after Ian Jamieson, their outside-left, had to retire from the field injured. The horror even reached 7-1 prior to Dave Curlett scoring in the 86th minute. That carnage at Alloa was the major contributory factor in the following week's game at home to Forfar Athletic being played in front of "the smallest crowd yet this season."

Mr Mays' job was made even more difficult when centre-half Jim McLean asked for a transfer in the wake of a defeat at Cowdenbeath on 17th February. The player then sat out four matches pending his sale to Dunfermline Athletic in March. He was their captain in the 1965 Scottish Cup final. Jacky McGugan was signed from Tranmere Rovers and he took over Jim McLean's shirt as well as the Ayr United captaincy. McGugan was a big gangly commanding player who had won the Scottish Cup with St. Mirren in 1959. His next club was Leeds United but he was starved of first team football by the form of eventual World Cup winner Jacky Charlton.

McGugan was just the type of leader Gerry Mays needed on the field. A late season flurry yielded three wins out of the last four league fixtures yet there was an inescapable conclusion that ninth place was a vast disappointment for a club that had just dropped out of the First Division. The public could not be blamed for their apathy. Sparse attendances were a clear indicator of public opinion.

Of the close season signings in 1962 the best was Johnny Kilgannon, who had been released by Stirling Albion. It said a great deal of Gerry Mays' powers of persuasion that he was able to tempt a player of such calibre to join a club which could no longer live off its reputation. This much was acknowledged in the *Ayr Advertiser's* report of a 3-0 win away to Albion Rovers on 29th September, 1962: "The acquisition of inside-forward Kilgannon was the smartest piece of work in the managerial

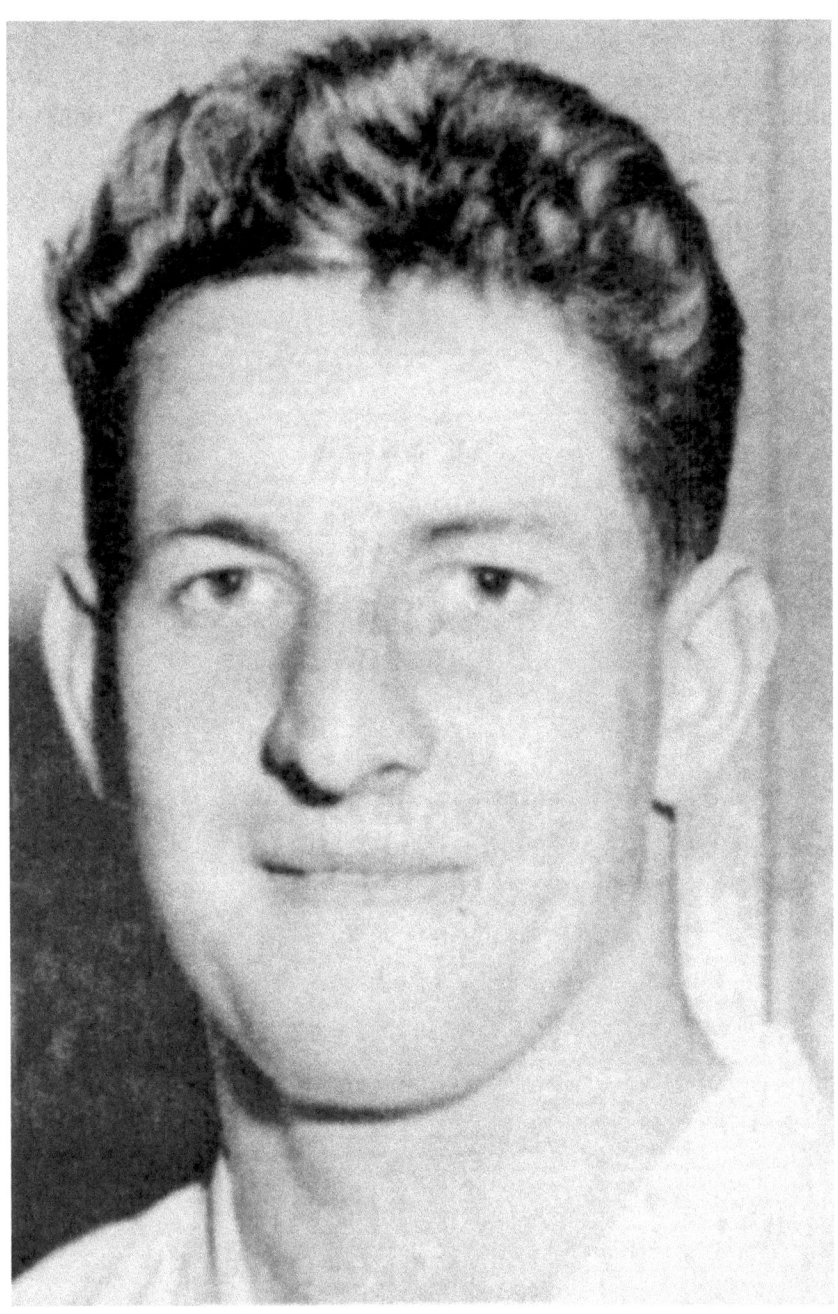

Johnny Kilgannon.

career of Gerry Mays at Somerset Park. And that's a fact." The report concluded with: "There was hardly a failure in the Ayr side." That evening the club sat second in the Second Division, separated from top club Stranraer merely on goal average.

Out of the next ten fixtures there was just one win but Mr Mays did not survive beyond the eighth game of that run. On the Tuesday evening of 4th December he handed in his resignation to the board.

Neil McBain

2. December 1962 – October 1963

You have just read about Gerry Mays resigning on a Tuesday. By the time Stranraer were at Ayr on the Saturday his replacement was installed. Neil McBain, deemed as a hero for restoring top grade football at Ayr in 1956, clearly bore no festering ill will against a club that wanted him to build on that success without a contract. Neilly was back. A 2-0 defeat on his return was reported as ending all promotion hopes. It was a superfluous comment. On that night of 8th December, 1962, eleventh place was occupied in the Second Division. One week later a 2-0 defeat away to Stenhousemuir prompted the *Ayr Advertiser* to describe it as "a performance almost as pathetic as the weather." The weather analogy was apt. That frozen winter of 1962/63 was heavily riddled with postponements and at the end of the elongated season the outcome was thirteenth place out of nineteen. Especially painful was a 7-2 thrashing at Stranraer on 13th April.

From personal testimony you can be told that even in 1963 the job of Ayr United manager had not yet cast off the dogsbody tasks of old. In the closing weeks of that season your writer and two friends turned up at Somerset Park one evening in the hope of watching Ayr United train. After nervously making our way through the entrance door Neil McBain appeared. He explained that the training was taking place at the Old Racecourse. We then agreed to his request to lift litter from the terracing for which we were paid with some silver from his own

The programme cover for the first match of Neil McBain's second stint as Ayr United manager. In the intervening years the cover had not been updated to show the changing kit. The kit shown here was similar to that used when he started his first stint in April 1955.

pocket. Even in later years the illustrious Ally MacLeod was charged with such mundane responsibilities as ordering pies.

Albion Rovers 3 Ayr United 1 – fifteenth place and two points off the bottom was the outcome on 26th October, 1963. This paled in comparison to the drama about to unfold in the boardroom. On the Tuesday night chairman Matt Pollock authorised secretary John Robertson to release a statement to the effect that Neil McBain had resigned. Yet Mr McBain was at his desk the next day and he denied that he had resigned. The issue had arisen in relation to a dispute with Jacky McGugan. Mr McBain had banned the player from the ground after his failure to keep his appointment with the trainer, Bob Cowie, in order to get treatment for an injury sustained against Stranraer. Gradually the untidy facts appeared. The board meeting had not taken place on the Tuesday. Five directors were there but, after a scene, two left. At this point Mr McBain was alleged to have resigned and the announcement was later made to a group of journalists. Forty-eight hours later directors Captain T.S. Kay and Samuel Neil left a board meeting, having carried out their intention to resign. William Paterson withdrew his resignation. That left five directors, the requisite number for a quorum. This was followed by another statement from John Robertson: "The board has regretfully accepted the resignation of directors Captain T.S. Kay and Mr Samuel Neil. Mr McBain has severed his managerial duties as from tonight and Mr Robert Flavell will take up his duties as manager immediately."

By this time he was marginally short of his 68th birthday and this makes him the club's oldest ever manager. He passed away on 13th May, 1974.

Bobby Flavell

2. October 1963 – December 1964

You have already read about the confusion surrounding the departure of Neil McBain. Once the confusion had been lifted it emerged that Mr Flavell had agreed to return to Ayr as manager. The first match of his second stint was a 2-1 defeat at home to Arbroath on 2nd November, 1963. A fortnight later he was surveying the wreckage of a 6-0 defeat against Clyde at Shawfield. The last Saturday in the year marked a 6-1 defeat at Berwick. 1964 would go down as the worst year in Ayr United's history. Fittingly the first four league games of the year were lost including a 5-1 trouncing at Alloa. On the morning of 18th January, Mr Flavell had major problems regarding team selection for the Queen's Park match at Hampden. The situation he faced was chronic and this was reflected in the team selection. Goalkeeper John Gallacher was selected at outside-right in place of flu victim Johnny Hubbard while back-up goalkeeper Alastair Paton appeared in goal. It was a stark illustration of the club's poverty of resources. The match was lost 3-2. Opposition goalkeeper Bobby Clark made some outfield appearances for Aberdeen in 1969/70 but these were tactical rather than enforced.

On 15th February, 1964, Ayr United turned up for a Scottish Cup tie at Aberdeen and the general expectation was a slaughter in favour of the home team. League form, or the lack of it, had sunk the club to joint third bottom of the Second Division. There would have been fans in the ground who could recall

Aberdeen winning 8-0 in Ayr United's previous Scottish Cup visit on 8th February, 1947. Mr Flavell opted for his favoured 4-2-4 formation and it seemed to work. Deep into the second half Aberdeen led merely by a 56th minute goal. Sensationally Kenny Cunningham smashed the ball into the roof of the Aberdeen net in the 77th minute. Even more sensationally Johnny Kilgannon scored in the 87th minute and the game was played out at 2-1. Never before had an Ayr United team won away from home in the Scottish Cup against a club from a higher league. During his tenure at Ayr this was the peak for Bobby Flavell. In the Scottish Cup quarter-finals the team found its default 1964 form and lost 7-0 at Dunfermline then limped to fourteenth place in the Second Division. Philosophically it could have been said that things could only get better. In truth it was to get a lot worse.

No points from the opening five league matches of 1964/65 did not even comprise the worst of the club's troubles. The *Scottish Sunday Express* dated 22nd November, 1964, carried an unnerving back page headline:

AYR UNITED MAY QUIT

When the *Ayr Advertiser* came out on the Thursday there was a front page headline which stoked the fears:

AYR UNITED BOARD LEAVE CLUB'S FUTURE IN THE HANDS OF THE FANS

A statement issued by the board confirmed the threat. The Sunday paper had said "a closedown looks imminent" and the local paper, in quoting the press release, said that "the length of time the club will be able to carry on depends upon the support it receives from the public of Ayr and district through the turnstiles and the Development Club." The expression 'catch 22' could have been made for this predicament. Survival was dependant on public support when the team was struggling and there was no money with which to improve.

On 5th December the team lost 5-0 away to Stirling Albion. This left Ayr United as the lowest placed league club in

Scotland. On Tuesday, 8th December, Bobby Flavell resigned, citing that he ran a pub in Airdrie and could not do justice to both jobs. Such was our status that running a pub carried a higher priority than managing Ayr United. He was soon back in management with Albion Rovers.

Lazily, the conclusion could be drawn that he was a failure at Ayr. Yet closer scrutiny reveals that he made a raft of signings which would propel the club to promotion by the end of the following season. For example, in the 1964 close season his signings included Charlie Oliphant, Eddie Monan, Alex McAnespie, Dick Malone and Arthur Paterson. Most pertinently he signed Ally MacLeod that summer and recognised his coaching potential. Another of his significant acquisitions was Eddie Moore whom he had captured in March 1964.

Bobby Flavell passed away in March 2005.

Tom McCreath

December 1964 – May 1966

In the first two decades of the club's history conspicuous success was achieved under the management of men who had little or no experience of playing football. We had Harry Murray when consecutive Second Division titles were won in 1911/12 and 1912/13. Then there was Lawrence Gemson who was the manager when what remains the club's highest league position was achieved. That was fourth place in the First Division of 1915/16. Then we had Archie Buchanan as the manager when the Second Division title was won in 1927/28. Tom McCreath too would fit the mould of winning the Second Division title despite the fact that he would never have been able to pass the 'show us your medals' test.

Bobby Flavell quit on Tuesday, 8th December, 1964. On the following Tuesday his replacement was named. With the club teetering on the brink of financial oblivion the remuneration was always going to be modest. The editorial in the match programme was refreshingly candid: "Although Tom McCreath is very keen on football he did not play much of it."

However he did play at juvenile level for Park Rovers. One of his team mates there was Charlie McGillivray, a centre-forward who had signed for Ayr United from Dreghorn Juniors in May 1930. McGillivray's next clubs were Celtic, Manchester United and Motherwell. Mr McCreath's playing career did not take him to such imposing grounds as Old Trafford or Celtic Park. In contrast he went on to play for Ayr Ailsa, Dalmellington

Left to right: John Paton, Tom McGawn and Lewis Thow. They helped to pull the club back from the brink of extinction.

United and Auchinleck Talbot. After retiring as a player he was not out of football for long. Along with some colleagues he helped to start up Kirkmichael Amateurs in his home village. With his joinery business in Maybole thriving he quit football again. Once more it was not for long. In August 1964 he became the trainer for Ayr United reserves and in December he was elevated to manager.

His first game was at Stranraer. Ominously Ayr United had lost there in each of the previous three seasons. The omens were accurate. Stranraer won 2-0. Albion Rovers won 3-1 at Ayr on Boxing Day and Queen's Park beat Ayr United 2-1 at Hampden on New Year's Day, a Friday. A 3-1 win at home to Queen of the South on the next day was far from the best thing to happen to Ayr United that weekend. A new infusion of capital took place.

It was announced that Tom McGawn, head of a firm of road hauliers, had bought out majority shareholder Matt Pollock. This was a relief for Mr Pollock, who was following the advice of his doctor to relinquish his position at the club. A mysterious Mr X had stirred takeover talk but the proposals of the anonymous character had fallen through. Mr McGawn had been on the board for more than a year and his takeover was quickly followed by news on the Tuesday that Bob McCall, an Ayr garage proprietor, and John Paton, founder of a radio and television business recently bought by British Relay, had become directors. On the next again Tuesday chairman William Paterson, a local butcher, quit. Mr McGawn became chairman and the new vice-chairman was former Ayr United player Lewis Thow. Malcolm McPhail also had his position ratified as a new director at the same meeting.

These rapid changes in the boardroom provided stability for Tom McCreath and everyone else with Ayr United at heart. Even in January season 1964/65 was little better than a lost cause but the threat of extinction had been averted. The league programme was wound up with Ayr United in second bottom place in the Second Division, a record low in the history of the club. There was the further ignominy of having to apply for re-election. From personal testimony you can be told that there was a confidence surrounding the club at this time. Ostensibly it was our worst season in history but it did not erode an optimism. On the Monday evening of 26th April there was a potentially testing Ayrshire Cup final at Kilmarnock. The combatants were Kilmarnock (crowned league champions two days earlier) versus Ayr United (the second lowest club in Scotland). The match was won by a Davy Paterson goal to nil and we could even afford the luxury of a missed penalty.

Early in July Mr McCreath made a statement that was dripping in defiance when considered against what had happened in the season recently finished. He said: "We have one ambition and that is to get back into the First Division." This was from a man who did not have it in his nature to make rash statements. Yet he was a master joiner not a master magician. How could he seriously entertain such an ambition? Just two close season signings were made. These were right winger Johnny Grant from Hibs and inside-forward Ian Hawkshaw from St. Johnstone. At the annual general meeting on 27th July, directors Matt Pollock and Alec Moffat did not seek re-election. Mr Moffat had been on the board since 1923.

On the Monday evening of 25th April, 1966, Mr McCreath made another quote: "With virtually the same staff we have taken the club from the bottom five right to the top." This was on the occasion of winning 4-0 away to Stenhousemuir to clinch the Second Division title. What he said was modestly understated. His reference to 'the bottom five' could have been 'the bottom two'. On that same evening at Ochilview Park he praised Ally MacLeod's contribution as coach.

On the Wednesday evening a human tide engulfed the field when East Fife were beaten 2-0 at Ayr in the season's last league fixture. Applying for re-election one year then becoming champions the next year! It was scarcely credible. Mr McCreath considered that the job was done and he stepped down as manager.

Ally MacLeod

1. May 1966 – November 1975

Ayr United were founded in 1910; however, Ally MacLeod was probably under the impression that the year of foundation dated to nearer the mid-sixties when he was at the root of a most remarkable transformation! He was to become the most influential manager in the club's history and, of course, the best. For Ayr United supporters there is simply no debate on the issue. It all began when he took up his position on Thursday, 5th May, 1966, after being appointed during the weekend before.

In an extraordinary quirk of fate Ayr United's greatest ever manager had the same birthday as the club's greatest ever player and they were born precisely a year apart. Ally MacLeod was born on 26th February, 1931, and Peter Price entered the world on the same date in 1932. Ally signed a professional contract for Third Lanark in the summer of 1949. His next club was St. Mirren whom he played for in season 1955/56 but it was a short stay. He was soon on the move to Blackburn Rovers. In 1960 they reached the final of the FA Cup which involved a Wembley meeting with Wolves. He excelled on the left wing but the match was lost 3-0.

On 12th August, 1961, he made his debut for Hibs in a League Cup sectional tie away to St. Johnstone. Then, in 1963/64, he was back playing for Third Lanark. On his release he signed for Ayr United in the summer of 1964 and was quickly given the captaincy. The only appearances he made for the club were in that initial 1964/65 season. There were twelve in the

Alex Ingram.

league, six in the League Cup and one in the Scottish Cup. He stayed in Clarkston at the time and his full-time job was as a representative for ICI. Even when he began to develop his role in coaching, the club's fragile financial state compelled him to keep his regular job.

Ally MacLeod's name is synonymous with longevity. His three terms of management at Ayr United totalled almost fifteen years, a span more than double that of his nearest rival. He amassed 214 league wins for the club, another statistic which leaves him without a close rival. His inspiration was such that such longstanding attachment to Ayr United was infectious. Willie Wallace was a good example. In that summer of 1966 he was appointed club trainer, a role defined as physio in a later age. He maintained that role for seventeen years (later returning in an emergency situation from October 1984 to January 1985).

In retrospect we can now see that the club's longest serving manager worked alongside the club's longest serving trainer. What about the club's longest serving player? That honour goes to left-back John Murphy, who signed in July 1963 and remained until his release at the end of season 1977/78. He played for no other senior club and it was not merely coincidence that the bulk of his career was spent under Ally's management.

Ally's first signing was striker Alex 'Dixie' Ingram from Queen's Park. With the exception of a year at Nottingham Forest he remained an Ayr United player from 1966 until 1977, thereafter playing for no other senior club. Another summer 1966 signing was wing-half Dougie Mitchell from Crosshill Thistle, originally with Ayr Albion and Leeds United. In November 1974 he was transferred to Partick Thistle; he once told the author that, after the move, he missed playing under Ally's management. He also told the author that morale at Ayr United was so high that players habitually turned up early for training. Stan Quinn was another who subscribed to the 'not the same without Ally' school of thought. He too was signed in that

Bobby Rough.

summer of 1966. Quinn was a small but hard (extremely hard!) centre-half acquired from Shettleston Juniors. Eventually he moved on to St. Mirren in July 1973. Football without Ally was a factor in his decision to quit playing in January 1974. Alex McAnespie was an Ayr United player from 1964 until 1978; he, too, witnessed the whole transformation at the club.

The picture is clear. Here was a man who inspired loyalty in his players and staff. That loyalty was reciprocated. What did the fans think of him? Just ask any Ayr United supporter who was our best manager ever. There will be no requirement to even ponder on the question.

A popular phrase in everyday speech is 'learning curve'. It implies an experience in which lessons were taught and subsequently applied in an advantageous way. For Ayr United season 1966/67 was a learning curve and a most acute one at that. It saw what remains our worst run of consecutive games without a win. This comprised the first twenty-eight league fixtures plus two League Cup ties and one in the Scottish Cup. Just twenty league goals were scored and to compound the shame the Scottish Cup defeat referred to was on the waterlogged ground of Highland League club Elgin City. The sole league win came as late as 8th April. This was a 1-0 win at home to St. Johnstone. At the final whistle there was a celebratory pitch invasion in which the players got mobbed. No away league wins was a sobering experience which did not happen again until 1994/95. The sudden elevation from second bottom of the Second Division into the First Division had been miraculous with almost the same squad of players but it had happened too rapidly to be able to consolidate in the higher sphere.

It would be futile to conduct further analysis of the wreckage of 1966/67. Dear reader, you can be assured that the story is about to get better – much better!

Ally was a disciple of attacking football. At the 'Player of The Year' function in 1988 his speech touched on the subject

Cutty Young.

of club records and he expressed the point that he had no interest in defensive records. Yet this viewpoint never deterred him from pursuing players who would make the Ayr United defence as impenetrable as possible. One such was goalkeeper Davy Stewart, who signed in the summer of 1967, having recently won the Scottish Junior Cup with Kilsyth Rangers. His reserved nature was in contradiction to his spectacular performances. Ally's nature was far from reserved. When there was competition from other clubs his powers of persuasion were most useful when selling the benefits of joining Ayr United. The same powers of persuasion were used to inspire confidence in his players. His dressing room rhetoric worked. Although using rhetoric to maximum effect he was tactically aware.

The wreckage of 1966/67 was not wholly repaired in a season. Fifth place in 1967/68 was the platform on which the impending success was built. On 23rd November, 1968, a 2-0 win at Stranraer was the first of eleven consecutive league wins. That win was halted with a scoreless draw at Stirling on 8th March, 1969. A win at Stirling would have meant equalling the club record twelve consecutive league wins in 1936/37. This was not used an additional incentive for winning simply because no one in 1969 was aware of this particular record. Not that an additional incentive was needed anyway. Ally's desperation to win was so great that, during the second half, he instructed right-back Dick Malone to push up to outside-right. The Stirling match was a four-pointer in the scrap to finish runners-up to eventual champions Motherwell. This pursuit of the second promotion place was successful but amidst the delirium there were prophets of doom who gloried in predicting that this promotion would go the same way as the last one. There was never a chance that Ally was going to let that happen. A stronger foundation was laid when it was confirmed that the club would have a team in the Scottish Reserve League.

Davy Stewart.

Consistency in team selection was attributable to Ally being loyal to the players who were loyal to him. Yet it was not blind loyalty. He had high standards which he expected to be followed. From this time the author can recall turning up at Somerset Park on Thursday evenings to book a seat on the Supporters' Association bus for the Saturday. Thursdays were training nights and this afforded a view of training sessions. The training matches were especially interesting. Ally took part in these but this did not prevent him from roaring disapproval at aspects he was unhappy with. The errant player would be named in a booming voice and some of those who were the subject of his wrath are now Ayr United legends. He had a loathing too of slack habits. There was a purpose in fining players who were untidy in the dressing room. He took the view that untidiness off the pitch could lead to sloppiness on the pitch. High morale and almost military discipline! There is no point in even trying to make sense of it all. It worked!

There are people who were not even born at the time who can recite the Ayr United team that started season 1969/70. As a reminder, should it be needed, that team was: Stewart, Malone, Murphy, Fleming, Quinn, Mitchell, Young, Ferguson, Ingram, McCulloch and Rough. The cost (or lack of it!) of building that team bears interesting scrutiny. Only three were signed from other senior clubs. They were Jacky Ferguson (free from Southend United), Alex Ingram (from Queen's Park whose amateur status meant no fee) and Bobby Rough (free from Dundee).

The comparisons with 1966/67 quickly melted away. First league win in April – not this time! This time it was in August. Hibs were beaten 3-0 at Ayr in the opening league fixture. The next home league fixture brought Rangers to Ayr. In the build-up Ally was defiant in the face of the Old Firm-centric media. His optimism was infectious but for some of the fans there was a worry that the team might not live up to his boasts. Why did anyone doubt that a part-time team built at no cost

John Murphy.

would fail to beat a side containing some of the most hyped-up professionals in the land? In front of a ground record crowd Rangers were beaten 2-1.

A constant irritation at this time was a lack of respect from the national media. Successes in this season and beyond continually brought forth a 'wee Ayr' label as in "Wee Ayr shock Rangers." And why the use of the word 'shock'? Ally had already told them that it was going to happen.

The 'wee Ayr' insults were in further use when we played Celtic in the League Cup semi-final. It was almost like a punishment for having the temerity to draw 3-3 with them after extra time on that October night. In the replay on the following Monday evening (again at Hampden) we surrendered a 1-0 lead to lose 2-1. It was still a most creditable showing against a team that would contest that season's European Cup final.

Ally's PR was brilliant. His team was playing well and he was intent on letting the world know it. For a 0-0 draw at home to Hearts on 19th October the crowd figure approached 11,000. Two days afterwards he played in a benefit match for Bryan Douglas of Blackburn Rovers. The Blackburn Rovers FA Cup final team of 1960 won 10-6 against an England XI and he scored twice.

His ability to bring out the best in his players resulted in international recognition for a few. That season Alex Ingram got selected to play for the Scottish League and under-23 selections were made in respect of Dick Malone and Davy Stewart.

The season was played out with no relegation fears. Fourteenth place could be deemed as unspectacular but there were wins which could not have been similarly defined.

Within weeks of the season's end John Doyle was signed. A teenaged winger from Viewpark Boys Guild sounded as if he may be a prospect. The normal logic would have been to allow him to settle into reserve team football in order to work towards a first team place. Such caution was an alien concept to Ally. Doyle was thrust straight into the first team. Propulsion from

Stan Quinn.

juvenile football to the First Division typified the belief he had in his players. Of necessity he had a tendency to be critical of his players during training but in public he portrayed them as stars. He left people with a strong urge to get out and watch Ayr United.

1970/71 ended with the identical league position as the season before. Once again Rangers were beaten at Ayr and once again the "wee Ayr" insults were found in print. Public interest in the club remained high. During 1970/71 a floodlighting system was completed at a cost of £18,000. The general public raised £12,201: 14s: 11d. Then, in the summer of 1971, a roof was erected to cover the terracing at the Somerset Road end. For this initiative the public had no direct involvement in the funding. Indirectly the public's involvement was putting cash down at the turnstiles.

A twelfth place finish in 1971/72 was good enough to qualify for the Texaco Cup, a cross border competition. The infrastructure continued to be improved upon in the summer of 1972. Somerset Park was returfed and a training ground was created at Craigie Park. If questioned on what the season ahead would hold, most fans would have opted for finishing comfortably ahead of the relegation places. This was the developing pattern and few would have had any complaints about it. Such expectations were about to be surpassed.

The visit of Rangers for the opening league game was daunting. In May they had won the European Cup Winners' Cup. To this we can factor in the fact that the Rangers team of this time had a very physical approach. Ally was clear in his pre-match talk. His express instructions were to keep a cool and calm approach and not get drawn into a physical contest. After the loss of an early goal John Doyle and Alex Ingram scored for a 2-1 win. The *Evening Times* report did not mention "wee Ayr". Some respect at last? Not at all! Their report referred to "little Ayr".

On a Tuesday evening in February, Scotland played England in an under-23 international at Rugby Park. John Doyle was in the starting line-up and his Ayr United team mate Davy Wells was an unused substitute. For the home internationals of 1973 John Doyle was in Willie Ormond's squad of twenty-two but did not play. However the conclusion can be drawn that players from supposedly "wee" clubs do not find themselves in international contention. Let us now dispense with the siege mentality to indulge in some of the glories of 1972/73.

Partick Thistle were beaten 5-1 at Firhill to take Ayr United into the Scottish Cup semi-finals for the first time in the club's history. The Hampden semi-final was lost 2-0 to Rangers on a night when there was surface water on the pitch. The Scottish Cup run combined with a sixth-place finish in the 18-club First Division to make it the best season in living memory.

Building morale came naturally to Ally but that did not deter earnest attempts at team bonding. In the summer of 1973 four matches were played in Newfoundland then three more in Brittany. Once again the league opener was against Rangers, a 0-0 draw at Ibrox being the outcome. One week later Alex Ferguson made his Ayr United debut at home to Morton. His autobiography contained some very illuminating comments on what it was like to play under Ally's management.

"Some might have been put off by the dream factory Ally carried in his head but I was stimulated by his bubbling enthusiasm. He had the same effect on many others and the team he built at Ayr United showed that he had an eye for character as well as ability. I enjoyed my time with him and had reason to be grateful that he had rescued me from the feeling of neglect which was closing in after I left Falkirk as a free agent."

On 27th October, 1973, the team stood to go top of the First Division in the event of beating Dundee at Dens Park and hoping that Celtic would beat top-placed Hearts at Tynecastle. Celtic duly obliged. At Dundee, John Doyle had to go off injured after being the victim of an extremely bad tackle. Tommy Gemmell was only booked for a challenge which should have seen him banned into oblivion. Alex Ferguson opened the scoring one minute into the second half. The match was ultimately lost 2-1 and Ally was left in a rage about the damage done to John Doyle. Yet his team had a formidable reputation, especially at home. In the whole of 1973 only Celtic and Rangers had league wins at Ayr and Rangers only managed a 1-0 victory with an 88th minute goal on the last Saturday of the year. Ally had transformed the place into Fortress Somerset. When opposition managers said that they did not like playing at Ayr they were not being patronising. It was the honest truth.

A 5-0 Scottish Cup win at Cowdenbeath was followed by a 7-1 win at Stranraer. In the quarter-finals at Tynecastle we were ten minutes away from reaching the semi-finals in consecutive seasons but had to be content with a 1-1 draw in front of a crowd of 17,219. The attendance at the midweek replay was 16,185. That tie was lost 2-1 after extra time although we did manage to take full league points off Hearts in 1973/74. The sixth place of the season before was very close to being repeated. That position was conceded to Hearts on goal difference so we finished seventh.

The opening match of season 1974/75 was a 3-1 defeat in a League Cup sectional tie away to Dundee United. Standards were so high that this defeat at one of the more formidable grounds in the country was described as a debacle. The *Ayr Advertiser* report emotively mentioned a "Tannadice tragedy." In the next sectional tie Celtic were beaten 3-2 at Ayr in midweek.

For the third year in a row the opening league fixture was contested against Rangers. A 1-1 draw at home made it two draws and an Ayr win in this particular series. Ally loved the media attention of matches against the Old Firm. He was an expert in making quotes which were designed to boost Ayr United's image. By 1974 the "wee Ayr" insults were a memory. 1974/75 saw the relegation battle moved to midtable. The two-league structure was being converted to three leagues in the following season. This meant that the cut-off for the new

Premier League was tenth place out of eighteen. After Aberdeen had been beaten 2-0 at Ayr on 8th February, Ally set a top ten safety target of thirty points. To reach the target it was merely required to take seven points (at two for a win) from the eleven remaining fixtures. Thirteen points were taken. It transpired that the seven-point target would not have been enough. The cut was made comfortably in finishing seventh.

Ally's lust for attacking football was satisfied in a return trip to Newfoundland. His players scored forty-nine goals in eight matches, including fourteen in one match. In the heavily more competitive environment of the newly instituted Scottish Premier League, Ayr United became a victim of the club's own success. Ayr United 3 Rangers 0 was the result on 11th October, 1975, despite the visitors progressing to win a domestic treble that season.

The prospect of Ally leaving Ayr United seemed inconceivable but by dint of his success it happened. The back of the *Ayr Advertiser* dated Thursday, 6th November, 1975, made for contented reading, the team having had a 2-0 home win over Motherwell on the Saturday. Yet this was negated by the front page story stating that Ally MacLeod was leaving Ayr United to become the manager of Aberdeen: "The directors agreed to release him at a meeting on Tuesday afternoon. At the request of the players he was at Rugby Park on Tuesday night but he will not be at Perth on Saturday." The Rugby Park reference was in relation to an Ayrshire Cup tie, the result being Kilmarnock 0 Ayr United 3. History would record that this was not goodbye. It was *au revoir* and not just because he would come back for future spells of management. He was back in a matter of weeks. On 29th November he occupied the visitors' dugout at Somerset Park to watch a John Doyle-inspired Ayr United beat Aberdeen 1-0 by courtesy of a John Murphy goal. Aberdeen sat below Ayr United in the table even prior to this match and, at the season's end, we were still above them.

Virtually a year to the day after his departure (6th November, 1976) his Aberdeen team beat Celtic 2-1 in the League Cup final. In the semi-final his team had beaten Rangers 5-1. The ability to inspire victory against the Old Firm was clearly a transferable skill.

In May 1977 he was appointed as manager of Scotland. Tartan Army veterans will tell you that there has never been a better time to support Scotland. His belief inspired the whole nation but it was not simply pointless euphoria. Beating England at Wembley on 4th June, 1977, was a massive morale booster ahead of the pursuit of World Cup qualification. That qualification was duly sealed by beating Wales at Anfield on 12th October that year.

For too many years the efforts to get him inducted to the SFA's Hall of Fame were ignored. Justice at long last prevailed on 17th October, 2015.

Sam McMillan

November 1975

It is anticipated that many readers will peruse the heading while thinking "I definitely don't remember Sam McMillan managing Ayr United." The explanation is that this book is pedantic enough to include interim managers.

He remains the youngest player to have taken part in a competitive match for Ayr United. Born on 14th August, 1937, he was aged 15 years 212 days when playing versus Queen's Park at Hampden on 14th March, 1953. That happened in an emergency situation. Manager Archie Anderson approached Ballochmyle Thistle for permission to field Sam in a match. Young Sam thought that he was being asked to play in a trial. It transpired that he proceeded to play in a league fixture. He had already played for Scotland at schoolboy level. Two of his caps were for matches against England at Wembley and Aberdeen. The other match was against Wales at Swansea. From juvenile football he progressed to Auchinleck Talbot ultimately moving to Ayr United from Irvine Meadow in the summer of 1955.

Between then and his last game on 29th April, 1968, he scored 127 goals, an Ayr United total surpassed only by Peter Price. In October 1969 he got presented with a statuette by the Scottish Players' Union. It was awarded annually to the person whom they considered to have made the best contribution to Scottish football without previously having been recognised. By this time he was a valued right hand man to Ally MacLeod and would remain so until the great man's departure.

Sam McMillan.

Replacing Ally MacLeod was always going to be a daunting task and in the weeks pending the new appointment Sam McMillan was in interim charge for four Premier League games. The results were St. Johnstone 0 Ayr United 1, Ayr United 2 Celtic 7, Ayr United 1 Hibs 3 and Dundee 2 Ayr United 2. After Alex Stuart stepped in as the new boss, Sam remained in a coaching role until August 1976, at which time he quit in what was described as "an amicable break." In an outstanding display of loyalty Ayr United was the only senior club he ever served.

Alex Stuart

November 1975 – September 1978

Alex Stuart was an Aberdonian who signed for Dundee as a full-back in 1958 and he remained at that club until 1969. These were halcyon years at Dens Park. Dundee became champions of Scotland in 1961/62 then proceeded to reach the semi-finals of the European Cup in the season ahead. Alex Stuart was not in the Dundee team when the title was clinched at Muirton Park, Perth, on 28th April, 1962, but he was heavily involved in the European Cup run. The semi-final was lost 5-2 on aggregate to AC Milan and he played in both legs. He was also in the Dundee team that lost 3-1 to Rangers in the 1964 Scottish Cup final but, more positively, he was in their winning team in the semi-final – 4-0 against Kilmarnock. After his release he signed for Dundee United for whom he made just three first team appearances in 1969/70. In November 1969 he stepped into management at Montrose.

In season 1975/76 Montrose had a fantastic run to the semi-finals of the League Cup. The sectional ties saw them win their group ahead of East Fife, Raith Rovers and St. Mirren. Then, in the quarter-finals, his team beat Hibs 3-2 on aggregate. This was a Hibs team that had won Ayr United's section. Conquering Rangers at Hampden then presented an insurmountable hurdle but people did take notice of the progress made by a thirty-five-year-old manager working with limited resources. The team went on to finish third in the league, just one place below that required to win promotion to the Premier League.

Alex Stuart.

However Alex Stuart was not there to witness this lofty finish. On Tuesday, 25th November, it was announced that he would be quitting Montrose with immediate effect in order to become the manager of Ayr United.

By a quirk of fate his first match in charge coincided with Ally MacLeod returning to Ayr with his Aberdeen team. A John Murphy goal secured a 1-0 home win. This was the first season of the Premier League and the pressure of two relegated from ten was especially formidable for a part-time squad. Beating Celtic 2-1 at Celtic Park was an especially outstanding result in the third last game but it still took a last game win at home to Motherwell to survive, an added bonus being a sixth-place finish.

During the 1976 close season Alex Stuart took his squad to a continent never before visited by the club. Twenty players travelled to Africa for three matches in Nigeria. Mr Stuart did not witness the only defeat. That was in the final match. He stayed in Lagos to organise the flight home while the squad flew 400 miles inland to play The Mighty Jets of Kaduna. Playing on grass about six inches long, the only goal of the match was a controversial penalty.

For players who made their living outside of football the pressure was back on at the start of the 1976/77 league programme. Alex Stuart too was part-time. His day job was as the head teacher at Symington Primary. Kilmarnock quickly got cut adrift. The threat of going down with them was real when faced with a highly formidable run of fixtures spanning March and April. These games were Rangers (away), Aberdeen (away), Dundee United (away), Hearts (away) then Motherwell (home). After drawing at Ibrox the next four were won. Despite the imbalance of away matches the fear of going down was averted with three games left. We finished eighth and Hearts got relegated for the first time in their history.

As had happened at Montrose, Mr Stuart's managerial success got noticed. The season had barely finished when

Dundee asked the Ayr United board whether he would be available to replace Davy White. On the face of it this was a tempting proposal from a club he must have had an affinity with. Within four weeks of this he was offered the chance to manage Aberdeen following Ally MacLeod's acceptance of the Scotland job. The chance to be Ally MacLeod's successor for a second time was also ostensibly tempting since Aberdeen was the city he was born and raised in. Mr Stuart turned Aberdeen down too. Lesser mortals might have used these approaches to demand a better salary in their existing job but he was not opportunistically inclined to do this.

The anticipated formidableness of survival materialised in 1977/78. Mr Stuart was tactically aware and in his time with Ayr United so far he had been an effective motivator even although he was, like most of us, less extrovert than Ally MacLeod. He was shrewd, intelligent and abhorred pessimism. A 0-0 draw at home to bottom club Clydebank on 25ᵗʰ February, 1978, prompted scathing comments amongst the fans and the media. Mr Stuart was more angry about the pessimism than the actual performance. He even saw fit to break off relations with the *Ayrshire Post*. His comments were: "I'm very upset by what has appeared in your paper. From now on you can scratch around to fill your pages but I won't be helping." Initially it was assumed that he was angry at comments by their sports editor Bob McKenzie. It was a wrong assumption. He was upset by the paper printing critical letters from supporters. Besides there was no softening of attitude from Mr McKenzie. In the weeks ahead he justifiably wrote: "The world and his whippet have written off Ayr United as First Division fodder."

To this point of the season we had won both of our home games against Celtic but it was getting to the stage where we could no longer live off past glories, even those from the recent past. After the Clydebank match we lost the next seven in the league, the slump being arrested with a 1-1 draw at Ibrox in front of a miserly attendance of 12,282. This was paltry considering

Rangers were successfully closing in on a domestic treble. Game three in that run of defeats was at home to St. Mirren on 18th March. It was dispiriting to study the Premier League table on that Saturday night. Survival was based on catching the third bottom club. That club was Celtic!

It came as no surprise to anyone (including the aforementioned whippet!) when the team did indeed go down with Clydebank.

That summer Mr Stuart travelled to Argentina for the World Cup. His motive was the opportunity to study training methods. On his return he said: "I studied the Germans very closely." It may be overly simplistic to argue that the plan would never work owing to his Ayr United squad not possessing the quality of the Germans. Regardless of which angle his initiative is debated from, it is fact that an early push for promotion did not remotely happen. After one win in the first seven league games the club sat third bottom, saved from the foot of the table on goal difference only.

Losing 5-2 at home to Dumbarton on 16th September was too much to bear for the fans and for Mr Stuart himself. His resignation was announced on the following Saturday morning. Chairman Myles Callaghan stressed that the board had not put pressure on him to quit. The same could not be said of the general public. Mr Stuart had even complained of fans congregating outside his Alloway home and shouting disparaging comments.

He left an important legacy. Historically Ayr United managers had been burdened by clerical work. Alex Stuart appointed Helen Nelson to undertake such duties, a role she fulfilled at the club with unfailing devotion for nineteen years until 1995.

By early October 1978 he was back in management at St. Johnstone. On 5th April, 1980, that club sacked him in the morning thereby causing them to travel to Ayr that day without a manager.

Ally MacLeod

2. September 1978 – December 1978

On the morning of 23rd September, 1978, Alex Stuart quit as Ayr United manager, even although there was a league fixture away to Clyde in the afternoon. Ally MacLeod was invited to a meeting with the Ayr United directors with a view to his return. It was a bold initiative considering that he was still the Scotland manager. He agreed to come back! Euphoria! By this time the club had slipped out of the Premier League into the First Division; his target was simply defined as getting Ayr United back into the top sphere. On the evening of 27th September a league visit by Arbroath attracted a media scrum. Ayr United 3 Arbroath 0 – The Messiah was back! From his first six league games just one point was dropped. Two of these games brought a winner in the last minute – at Stirling and, more satisfyingly, at Kilmarnock. The faltering start to the season was forgotten and the self-belief was almost tangible. On consecutive October Saturdays there was a 6-4 win at Montrose then a 4-3 win at home to Clydebank. The attacking emphasis was once again in evidence.

The early evening news bulletins on Tuesday, 12th December, relayed a story that Ally MacLeod had agreed to manage Motherwell. Quite candidly it came as a shock. Nevertheless he had not seen the last of the manager's office at Somerset Park. The task of keeping Motherwell in the Premier League was too great. Ultimately a failure to get that club back out of the First Division cost him his job in 1981. On 23rd February, 1980, his

Motherwell team won 5-0 at Ayr. His next league visit to Ayr was on 9th August that year and the score was reversed. It was an ample illustration of just how erratic fortunes in football can be.

George Caldwell

1. December 1978 – January 1979

In late August 1976 Alex Stuart approached George Caldwell to enquire whether he would fill the coaching vacancy created by the departure of Sam McMillan. It just had to be a tempting offer. He had been the manager of Albion Rovers and was now being given a chance to work in the Premier League. Moreover he was a Catrine man. He had been an outstanding right-back in his day. He played in the Glenafton Athletic team that lost 2-1 to Irvine Meadow in the 1963 Scottish Junior Cup final. By the start of 1963/64 he was signed by Airdrie where he remained for a decade. In 1973/74 he was at St. Mirren and then he made the move to management at Albion Rovers.

When Ally MacLeod returned in September 1978 he found that George Caldwell had since replaced Sam McMillan as assistant manager. Ally preserved the status quo. Then, on quitting for Motherwell in December that year, Mr Caldwell was appointed manager on an interim basis. Ayr United 5 Montrose 0 – what a start! Maintaining such momentum was an impossibility and the month was played out with a 3-1 defeat at Clydebank and a 1-0 win away to Queen of the South, who were also operating with an interim manager. Every competitive match in January 1979 suffered a postponement. These comprised four league fixtures and a Scottish Cup tie which was postponed twice in January and twice more in February. An inconsequential Ayrshire Cup tie provided the only match practice that month. By the time winter had grudgingly released its grip Willie McLean was in charge and he kept George Caldwell on as his assistant.

George Caldwell.

Willie McLean

January 1979 – April 1983

Mr McLean accepted the Ayr United managerial vacancy in late January 1979. He could reflect on a career as a winger starting with his local club Larkhall Thistle, then Airdrie, Sheffield Wednesday, Alloa Athletic, Queen of the South, Clyde, Alloa Athletic again and Raith Rovers. His managerial career had spanned Queen of the South, Motherwell, then Raith Rovers - whom he was quitting to move to Somerset Park. At this time his brother Jim was managing Dundee United and his brother Tommy was playing for Rangers.

January 1979 was plagued with postponements then, on 3rd February, Ayr United took part in the club's first league fixture of the year. This was Willie McLean's first match in charge. It was a 3-1 defeat at Hamilton's Douglas Park. He learned from this and the transformation was immediate. Full points were taken from the next four league fixtures which included consecutive 5-0 wins (Montrose at home, Clyde away) and a morale boosting midweek win at home to Kilmarnock. The derby win put us level on points with top-placed Kilmarnock and we had the luxury of a game in hand. Erratic form in the run-in created a stuttering fourth place.

The attempt to immediately return to the Premier League having failed, there was still enough confidence to entertain promotion hopes in 1979/80. By the fifth match we had all been disabused of that notion with just one point taken and bottom place being occupied. The dissent from the terraces was loud

Willie McLean with the British Oxygen Cup, which was won in the summer of 1979 after finishing top of a mini-league containing Elgin City, Keith and Clyde.

and bitter. Losing 6-2 at Airdrie then 3-0 at home to Hamilton Accies required drastic action from Mr McLean. Further aggravating the situation was the sale of Brian McLaughlin to Motherwell for £100,000 on the Tuesday. Yet by way of balance that transaction was preceded by the purchase of Eric Morris and Davy Armour from Rangers for a combined fee of £50,000. For the game against Dunfermline Athletic that night the Somerset Park attendance was described as "a pitiful crowd of only 1,668". All of the transfer business had been conducted within hours of the kick-off and fans entered the ground to be puzzled by the sight of two Ayr United players whom they did not recognise. Eric Morris scored four minutes into his debut and Derek Frye, signed from Dundee United the month before, found the net twice in a 3-0 win.

After losing 1-0 at Clydebank in the next game the team went unbeaten in the next sixteen league fixtures. This was just one short of the club record seventeen consecutive league games unbeaten in 1958/59. The assault on the record fell on the return visit to Clydebank on 12th January, 1980. That defeat meant that fourth place was maintained. On the evening of 1st April a 1-0 win away to leaders Hearts was an outstanding result but the enthusiasm was tempered by being too far behind them. Even the second promotion place was an unlikely hope. Five points behind Airdrie with five games to play! At two points for a win promotion hopes lived only in the heads of extreme optimists. Finishing third was an achievement in itself when considered against an awful start.

To Willie McLean's credit he was instrumental in seeing that the momentum rolled on into 1980/81. The season opened with a 1-0 win away to Celtic in the Drybrough Cup. Eight days later FA Cup holders West Ham United only managed a 1-1 draw at Ayr with a last minute goal. Then the league programme started with a 5-0 at home to Motherwell. This remains a club record winning margin in an opening league fixture (shared with Queen's Park 1 Ayr United 6 in 1921). In the League Cup

Morton, Queen of the South, Hearts and Hibs were beaten on the way to the semi-finals. All of the conquered clubs were in the Premier League with the exception of Queen of the South. Hearts got obliterated 7-2 on aggregate. Only Archie Anderson (1950) and Ally MacLeod (1969) had managed Ayr United to this stage of the competition. Dundee won 4-3 on aggregate in ties played on 5th and 19th November, 1980, but by January we had beaten them home and away in the league. On Sunday, 25th January, 1981, Ayr United chairman Myles Callaghan was approached by Kilmarnock who were seeking permission to talk to Willie McLean with a view to filling their managerial vacancy. On the Monday morning there was a board meeting at Somerset Park in order that the situation could be discussed with Mr McLean. After the meeting Mr Callaghan commented: "I am delighted to say that Willie McLean is staying at Ayr." This message was passed to the Kilmarnock board who promptly moved to appoint Jim Clunie.

After a 1-0 defeat at Motherwell on 11th April, Willie McLean said: "To finish fifth or sixth in Division One is a disgrace to a club of our calibre." Two fixtures later the programme was wound up with the club sixth.

In one of the League Cup sectional ties at the start of the 1981/82 season Premier League Partick Thistle were beaten 5-1 on their own ground, Derek Frye scoring four past Alan Rough, who was then the Scotland goalkeeper. Beating Motherwell home and away and Partick Thistle home and away was not enough to win the group. It was topped by Dundee United who were managed by Willie McLean's brother Jim. Dundee United were on course to retain the trophy.

Although failing to progress the form shown could not be faulted. Losing twice by a single goal to one of Scotland's best teams was far from discouraging. With the onset of the league programme there were few signs of slackening standards. It took until the thirteenth fixture of 1981/82 for the club to taste the first league defeat. That happened at Clydebank on 31st October but that evening we sat in second place just two points behind

Motherwell. A Scottish Cup defeat at Alloa on 30th January, 1982, was a crushing disappointment. Willie McLean said: "It is the biggest disappointment I have ever suffered in football."

On beating Clydebank at Ayr on 6th February, Ayr United remained in second place but Motherwell now had a lead of eight points. None of the next ten league games was won, including two against East Stirling. Even when the drought ended there was a lot of anger. The match in question was won 1-0 by an Alan McInally goal after twenty-three seconds. It could so easily have been lost because visitors Falkirk contrived to miss two second half penalties in the space of two minutes. During the match a posse of fans mounted a loud and angry protest. Willie McLean considered it a display of vehemence that affected the team's performance. This critical section of the crowd (of which the author was part) moved to an area near the home dugout. It must have been unsettling for the management team. The penultimate league fixture at home to Queen of the South resulted in a 5-2 win before a critically low attendance of 863. In time a sixth-placed finish in the second sphere would be considered a good season but in 1982 it was simply awful.

On losing 1-0 at home to Dumbarton on 13th November, 1982, Ayr United sat in second bottom place. Even when the Scottish Cup came round there was no respite. One year after losing at Alloa there was the ignominy of losing 2-1 at home to Albion Rovers. In reference to the Albion Rovers defeat the *Ayr Advertiser* commented: "Thousands of fans have already had enough; many more will follow them away from the terracing unless something is done quickly." On 9th April, 1983, Dunfermline won 3-2 at Ayr in a relegation four-pointer. The crowd, if it can be defined thus, was barely 700. There was a post match demonstration in Tryfield Place, in which the author was once more part. Mr McLean resigned on the Monday evening and it was left to his assistant, George Caldwell, to pull the club out of the relegation mire.

In season 1984/85 he was manager of Morton.

George Caldwell

2. April 1983 – October 1985

With relegation to the third tier looking like a distinct possibility Willie McLean resigned on Monday, 11th April, 1983. Once more George Caldwell found himself in interim management of the club. There is an old saying about being thrown in at the deep end. That was precisely the situation here. Five games were left, the first two of which were lost at Alloa then at Hamilton. Ironically the scorer in the 1-0 defeat at Hamilton was Brian McLaughlin. This was the same player who had scored four in the rout of Montrose that had comprised Mr Caldwell's first foray into Ayr United management back in 1978. It was just too bad that McLaughlin was now wearing the red and white of Hamilton Accies rather than the black and white of Ayr United. In fact it was more than too bad. The situation was now chronic. With three fixtures left the club was second bottom of a league from which two would go straight down. Alan McInally scored a hat-trick in a 4-0 win at home to Queen's Park then Robert Connor scored a hat-trick when Raith Rovers were beaten 3-2 at Ayr a week later.

The key fixtures on the last Saturday were Clyde versus Ayr United and St. Johnstone versus Dunfermline Athletic. Queen's Park were already doomed. St. Johnstone winning would keep Ayr safe even in the event of defeat at Shawfield. In the event that St. Johnstone did not win they were at risk of conceding the league title to Hearts so we were fortunate that they had something to play for. Danny Masterton then Pat Nevin put

Clyde 2-0 ahead by the 64th minute. The match was ultimately lost 3-2. At 1-0 to St. Johnstone relegation was averted. Relief was mixed with feelings that we should never have had to rely on other clubs. As for George Caldwell he had succeeded in the task set for him. In the last week of May 1983 he accepted the job of manager on a permanent but part-time basis. He brought in his old Airdrie team mate Derek Whiteford as his assistant. Mr Whiteford had managed Albion Rovers for a short spell in the season recently completed and he was a nephew of Jock Whiteford, a centre-half who had signed for Ayr United from Rutherglen Glencairn in May 1939.

There was consensus amongst the fans that the last day escape of 1982/83 should not be repeated in 1983/84. Mr Caldwell was like minded on this point. However the nerves would again be shredded with an even more uncomfortable escape. The management team had close links with Albion Rovers and this was to contribute in no small measure to survival in the First Division. Midfielder Gerry Collins was acquired from Albion Rovers for a small fee. He was a gritty midfielder, then aged twenty-eight. The *Ayr Advertiser* was soon reporting that: "Gerry Collins is adding strength to the midfield – a department which has let Ayr United down often in the past."

The last fixture of the season was at Dumbarton on 12th May, 1984, and again the permutations were being studied. Alloa Athletic were already relegated and either Raith Rovers or Ayr United would join them in the drop. We had a one point advantage over Raith but their fixture, Meadowbank Thistle away, was less formidable. Dumbarton were already promoted to the Premier League but a win over Ayr would be enough to go up as champions if Morton were to lose at home to Kilmarnock. Assuming a Raith Rovers win (it happened!) Ayr United had to beat a Dumbarton team high on incentive. Gerry Collins headed a wonderful double in the closing minutes of the first half. Alan McInally made it 3-0 with a superb solo goal when the game was drawing to a close. Afterwards Mr Caldwell was lavish in his praise of the backing from the fans.

The 'it must never happen again' scenario had happened again! Saved on the last day! If it was going to go right down to the wire for a third consecutive season it would surely be time to replenish the stock of footballing clichés. The Ayr United players were the best customers in that last chance saloon but it appears that the Honest Men were barred from the premises in 1984/85. Seventh place out of fourteen was midtable bliss.

Palpable progress removed the trepidation in the summer of 1985. Mr Caldwell announced that Gerry Collins would be the captain in 1985/86. League fixture number three was a 3-0 win at home to Kilmarnock and this match coincided with the return of prodigal son Hugh Sproat to the club. There were no outward signs of discontent therefore it came as a shock when George Caldwell resigned on the Monday evening of 21st October. East Fife had been beaten 1-0 at Ayr on the Saturday. That match was also the last Ayr United match played by Gerry Collins. He was sold to Hamilton Accies for £7,500 and went straight into the team for a 2-0 win against Ayr at Douglas Park.

In reference to his resignation Mr Caldwell said: "There were a few words said on Saturday night that I got upset at."

Davy Wells

1. October 1985

It may be that readers do not recall Davy Wells having had one spell of management at the club far less two. Both stints were on an interim basis. At the age of seventeen he signed for Ayr United from Auchinleck Talbot during the 1970 close season. Displacing Dick Malone from the right-back position was a formidable prospect for a young player. The sale of Malone to Sunderland in October 1970 at least opened a window of opportunity. Ally MacLeod said: "Davy Wells is going to be a great full-back in the Malone mould." He was nevertheless left to learn his craft in the reserve team until making a league debut at home to Cowdenbeath on 17th April, 1971. In 1971/72 he was again a regular in the reserves but this was not an ordinary reserve team. Ayr United became the reserve champions of Scotland that season. 1972/73 was an outstanding season for the club in general and Davy Wells in particular. On 13th February, 1973, he was an unused substitute for Scotland in an under-23 international against their English counterparts. The mere fact that he was in the squad said a lot about a player who had yet to complete a full season of regular first team football. By 1978/79 he was the team captain but in 1979/80, his tenth at the club, he lost his place to Billy McColl. At the end of that season he was released and his next club was Glenafton Athletic.

In March 1984 Derek Whiteford quit as assistant to George Caldwell after agreeing to become part of a new management team at Dumbarton. Davy Wells was successful in his

Davy Wells.

application for the vacancy created. When George Caldwell resigned Davy Wells was named as interim manager. On 26th October, 1985, Ayr United lost 2-0 away to Hamilton Accies and his caretaker spell began and ended with this one match. This was not a slight on his capabilities. It was because of the return of the incomparable Ally MacLeod.

Ally MacLeod

3. November 1985 – December 1990

By 1984/85 he was managing Airdrie and on the Friday evening of 1st November, 1985, he was announced as the new Ayr United manager in succession to the recently departed George Caldwell. Quitting Airdrie and taking over at Ayr happened inconveniently close to the home match with Partick Thistle the next day. After surveying a 3-1 defeat his analysis was: "There is a lot of work to be done." Ally was not renowned for understatement but neither was this comment an overstatement. There was too much work to be done. Relegation along with bottom club Alloa Athletic was the outcome. 1986/87 was to be spent in the third tier, ambiguously known as the Second Division.

On 9th May, 1987, just one point from the final league game was needed for promotion. The result was Ayr United 2 Stirling Albion 3. Lessons were learned and ruthlessly applied. In the campaign ahead there would be no reliance on the last game.

Season 1987/88 saw a return of the Ally of old. He was heavily optimistic and the swashbuckling style of his favoured attacking abandonment was once more in evidence. In storming to the league title sixty-one points were amassed, a club record based on two points for a win. St. Johnstone also amassed enough points for what was their own club record but it could only win them a runners-up spot. The *Daily Record* offered a crate of champagne to the first team to score 100 goals in all competitions. After winning the prize Ally offered to match it if the team reached 150. Four games were left! The idea of getting

Ally MacLeod in the dugout for the first match of his third managerial stint at Ayr United. From left to right the others are Jim McDonald, Jimmy Murphy and Davy Wells.

back into the second sphere had no fears. It is true that season 1988/89 had some great moments. After taking a 4-1 lead at home to Kilmarnock on 3rd January, Ally was content for his team to play out time while emphasising their superiority in other ways. It was not a coincidence that players such as John Sludden and Henry Templeton played the best football of their careers at Ayr. They were managed by a character who knew how to get the best out of them. Nevertheless that first season back in the First Division was more testing than expected. It took until the penultimate league fixture to guarantee survival. The club reverted to full-time contracts in time for 1989/90 but the expected progress was modest – eleventh to tenth.

In December 1990 Ally was told that his contract would not be renewed in June 1991. That prompted him to make the break straight away. His last game in charge was Ian McAllister's testimonial on the night of 11th December.

He managed Queen of the South in 1991/92, even playing for them in a reserve match against their St. Mirren counterparts at the age of sixty-one. On the night of 28th July, 1993, the Ally MacLeod testimonial match was staged at which time he was the commercial manager of Airdrie. Appropriately the opposition was supplied by Blackburn Rovers who travelled north to beat Ayr United 1-0. It was a decent result considering that, in the season about to start, Blackburn Rovers would finish as runners-up to Manchester United in the Premiership. One season later they would actually win the Premiership.

When his long career was behind him he regularly attended matches at Somerset Park. Understandably he was always well received.

He passed away on 1st February, 2004, at the age of seventy-two. His funeral was massively attended. Blackburn Rovers legends were there as was Manchester United boss Alex Ferguson.

A popular epitaph is 'Gone but not forgotten'. These words neatly sum up his passing.

Davy Wells

2. December 1990 – January 1991

Mr MacLeod's departure in December 1990 left Davy Wells as interim manager pending a permanent appointment. As assistant manager he was the obvious short term successor once more. With the visit of Airdrie on 15th December he was re-immersed in management in a 2-2 draw. One week later there was a 2-0 win at Clydebank and one week further Morton were beaten 1-0 at Ayr. Five points from a possible six and, but for a late Airdrie penalty, it would have been three straight wins. Kilmarnock's visit on 2nd January, 1991, seemed winnable on the basis of historical precedent. They had not won a New Year match at Ayr since 1967. In front of a crowd of 9,448 the trend was upset in a 2-1 defeat. In these four matches Davy Wells acquitted himself well in management and he was kept on as assistant to George Burley until the end of the season when Dale Roberts replaced him as the number two. In his post-footballing days he ran his own newspaper shop in Prestwick.

George Burley

January 1991 – December 1993

When George Burley applied for the job of Ayr United manager his CV was impeccable. He was a native of Cumnock who had played for Ayr Boswell at youth level before setting out on a glowing career. In suggesting that he was an outstanding right-back there is no patronising intent. On 29th December, 1973, he made his first team debut for Ipswich Town against Manchester United at Old Trafford. He played in the Ipswich team which defeated Arsenal in the 1978 FA Cup final and was most unfortunate to miss the 1981 UEFA Cup final. Ipswich Town beat AZ Alkmaar over two legs to win the trophy but he was kept out by a knee injury. In 1983 he had a testimonial match versus Aberdeen and he went on to play for Sunderland, Gillingham and Motherwell, whom he was now leaving to join Ayr United. In addition to eleven full Scotland appearances he had also represented his country at schoolboy, under-21 and under-23 levels. This impeccable CV was matched by equally impeccable references from Bobby Robson, Iain Munro, Andy Roxburgh, Jim McLean and Tommy McLean.

A mid-season appointment can indicate dissatisfaction with the status quo. Here was a thirty-four-year-old manager with fresh ideas and with the bonus of still being a good player. His first game in charge was a 1-0 defeat away to Meadowbank Thistle on 12th January, 1991. He played in that match and thereafter appeared as the regular right-back. One week later the world was a beautiful place once more. At home to Brechin

Duncan Carmichael, Ally MacLeod and George Burley.

City the half-time lead was 4-0. So was the lead at time-up but there was no meaningful grumbling at the second half lull.

Mr Burley had the foresight to pluck striker Ally Fraser from the reserves. In the last minute of a Scottish Cup replay at Hamilton he headed the winner then proceeded to score four in a 5-3 win at home to Raith Rovers on the Saturday. Mr Burley had a liking for professionalism. Training was well regimented and even the pre-match warm-up had an organised look to it. This semblance of order did not always manifest itself in the results. 1990/91 concluded with the club third bottom. With two going down automatically this position was greeted with relief rather than frustration.

On Monday, 20th May, 1991, Dale Roberts took over from Davy Wells as assistant manager. Dale Roberts, aged thirty-four, had been a team mate of George Burley at Ipswich Town. As a central defender he had played for England at youth level. In February 1980 he was sold to Hull City for £70,000 but a pelvic injury cut short his playing career at the age of twenty-eight. He then became a coach with Bridlington Town before returning to Hull City as a youth coach. His next move was to Ayr United. Dale Roberts knew the game well and he was excellent when it came to articulating his views on local radio. In future years he would team up with George Burley at Colchester United then at Ipswich Town again. In 2003 he died at the tragically young age of forty-six but here in 1991 it looked as if Ayr United had a management team with the capability of achieving conspicuous progress.

As soon as season 1991/92 was underway it was evident that fitness levels were high. The first four league fixtures were won, a feat not achieved since 1958/59. In the League Cup, Dundee were beaten 4-2 at Dens Park after extra time. Stamina levels were so high that extra time could have been perceived as an advantage. St. Johnstone, of the Premier League, were beaten 2-0 at home in the next round and progress was halted in the quarter-finals when Hibs won by the same score at Ayr on

Greg Shaw.

their way to winning the League Cup. When a player-manager is not the captain it could raise the question of who has the authority on the pitch. This was a phase when George Burley was well respected as a manager but Willie Furphy, in his role as captain, did not hesitate to issue verbals at him in moments of slackness.

Ayr United 7 Meadowbank Thistle 0 was achieved in appalling weather conditions comprising high winds and heavy rain. It was the first time we had scored seven in a competitive match since winning 7-1 in a Scottish Cup tie at Stranraer on 16th February, 1974. At home we had last scored that number in a 7-1 win over Stenhousemuir in a league fixture played on 19th October, 1968. After this annihilation of Meadowbank Thistle no Ayr United team scored seven in a competitive match again until 19th September, 1998, when Stranraer were beaten 7-1 in the league. The fans were buoyant due to the manner in which Meadowbank Thistle were beaten. In good numbers they headed to Greenock a week later. Morton led 3-1 until a turnaround with goals from Greg Shaw (78), Paul McLean (82) and Ian McAllister (stoppage time). In winning 4-3 there was no element of luck. To this point of the season (including the Morton match) nine goals had been scored in the 82nd minute or later.

On 8th December, 1991, the B & Q Cup final was lost 1-0 to Hamilton Accies at Fir Park, Motherwell. A year earlier we had lost 3-2 to Dundee after extra time in the inaugural final when it was known as the Centenary Cup. The single-goal defeat on each occasion should not be allowed to mask the fact that the supreme effort of 1990 was not replicated in 1991. Attitudes were questionable.

13th February, 1992, was a Thursday and on that day Steve Archibald phoned George Burley to ask about the possibility of getting a game. He trained with Ayr United that evening and then again on the Friday morning. Now aged thirty-five, the ex-Spurs and Barcelona striker looked sharp and he was

Gregg Hood.

included in the team that faced Partick Thistle at Firhill on the Saturday. In the 78th minute he went off with a groin strain and was replaced by Greg Shaw. He did not play for Ayr United again but a week later Mr Burley made it clear that his younger players would be getting a chance for what remained of the season. In truth there was quite a lot of the season left but the conclusion was reasonably drawn that promotion to the Premier League was a lost cause for 1991/92. Finishing sixth was not what was envisaged during the early season onslaught. There were a couple of redeeming features. Discipline was good. Throughout the entire season not one Ayr United player was sent off during first team action. The other redeeming feature was the strength of the youth team. On 15th April, 1992, the Ayr United youth team played their Hibs counterparts in the final of the BP Youth Cup. This Ayr team was managed by John Connolly and there was a distinct disadvantage in the choice of the venue – Easter Road! Still, it did attract an attendance of 6,562 which was then a record for the competition. The final was lost 2-0 but there were good prospects in the team, most notably Derek Allan and Gregg Hood.

The opening weeks of season 1991/92 were spectacular. In contrast the opening weeks of 1992/93 were spectacularly bad. The first eight league fixtures yielded just one win. Perhaps the use of the word 'just' should be reviewed. It was a 2-0 home win against Kilmarnock. After losing at home to Cowdenbeath on 12th September, 1992, we remained second from the foot of the table. George Burley had been omitting himself from the team. This was soon proven to be a mistake. The next match was at Dumbarton and he selected himself at right-back. He made a crucial difference. The 2-0 half-time lead came from headed goals from Ally Graham then John Traynor. Both came from Burley crosses. In stoppage time he crossed to Gordon Mair who laid the ball off to Alan McTurk who curled a neat shot into the net for a 3-0 result. George Burley was heavily involved in all of the goals.

On 6th February, 1993, there was a heavy media presence at Somerset Park. 13,918 tickets were sold for a fourth round Scottish Cup tie against Rangers despite the actual attendance numbering 13,176. The tie was lost 2-0 but the Tennents Man of the Match award went to George Burley rather than one of the players in the expensively assembled Rangers team. In the league run-in the terraces assumed a ghostly appearance in comparison to this cup tie. On 6th March merely 1,270 were tempted to attend a home match against Cowdenbeath. When promotion and relegation both become unlikely contingencies the result is likely to be a degree of apathy. Seventh place was all that could be mustered. For what little it was worth Ayr United had more league draws (eighteen) than any other club in that league.

1993/94 brought added pressure with it. From 1994/95 the system in Scotland was changing from three leagues to four leagues of ten. These would be designated Premier, First, Second and Third. It meant that, at the end of the season ahead, only one club would step up from the First Division to the Premier Division and five would drop into the Second Division. The one club emerging from the Second Division would round it off to ten. To make the cut Ayr United would need to finish no lower than seventh out of twelve.

George Burley could always be relied upon to be thorough in his preparation but then we all know what Rabbie Burns said about the best laid plans. The season opened with a 6-0 defeat at home to Motherwell in the League Cup. Excepting the Arsenal friendly it was our biggest home defeat since Dundee United had won 7-0 at Ayr on 24th September, 1966. It also marked our 100th defeat in the 272 League Cup ties played by Ayr United. Furthermore it remains our heaviest League Cup defeat of all time.

Losing at home to Airdrie on 13th November had the effect of plunging the club into the dreaded bottom five. These were nervous times and a 6-1 defeat at Dunfermline on the night of

14th December caused Mr Burley to condemn his players for a lack of fighting spirit. That was on the Tuesday. On the Saturday the Ayr United left-back for a home match with Falkirk was Arthur Albiston. He has the distinction of being the first player to win the FA Cup with Manchester United three times. Even at the age of thirty-six his appearance in an Ayr United shirt was a shock. His career at Ayr began and ended with this match. A Falkirk team containing eventual Ayr United manager Ian McCall won 3-0 and there was an angry reaction from the crowd. In the league table we slipped from seventh to eighth, overtaken by Stirling Albion.

On the Thursday evening of 23rd December, 1993, George Burley was sacked along with Dale Roberts. Mr Burley had been in charge of the club for 128 league games of which forty-three were won, forty-one drawn and forty-four lost. He was immediately offered training facilities with Falkirk and even played for them at Hamilton on 8th January, 1994. There was strong speculation that he was on the point of signing for Clydebank but this was wayward. After his brief association with Falkirk he rejoined Motherwell. On 1st June, 1994, he was appointed as manager of Colchester United after quitting his player-coach role at Motherwell. Colchester is located eighteen miles from Ipswich, a place he had a strong affection for and in December 1994 he was appointed as manager of Ipswich Town. He failed to save that club from relegation from the Premier League in 1994/95 but he did succeed in getting Ipswich back into that hallowed sphere in 2000. In that first season back he guided them to fifth place. It was a feat that won him the PFA Manager of The Year award. As if to illustrate the fickle nature of football they got relegated the next season. From 2003 until 2005 he managed Derby County then he moved north to manage Hearts in the summer of 2005. At Hearts he won eight of the first ten league games. The author can recall driving to Dumbarton on 22nd October, 2005, and hearing on the radio that Burley was no longer the Hearts manager. It was difficult to comprehend. Hearts topped the league. The reason given was "irreconcilable differences." On 23rd December, 2005, he succeeded Harry Redknapp as manager of Southampton. This was the twelfth anniversary of his sacking by Ayr United. Gareth Bale, Theo Walcott and Adam Lallana all made their senior debuts under George Burley at Southampton. On 24th January, 2008, he quit the south coast in order to manage Scotland. He was dismissed from the national job on 16th November, 2009. The following summer he accepted the manager's job at Crystal Palace but he was dismissed after half a season. During his brief tenure he gave a first team debut to Wilfried Zaha. Between May and September 2012 he experienced a further stint in management with Apollon Limassol in Cyprus.

Simon Stainrod

December 1993 – September 1995

George Burley was dismissed on the night of 23rd December, 1993, and Simon Stainrod was named as his successor on the same night. Earlier on the same day David Kennedy, then Ayr United's longest serving player, was sold to Queen of the South. For those at the administrative heart of the club Christmas preparations were put on hold. Simon Stainrod's arrival was greeted with euphoria. This was partly because his character was similar to that of Ally MacLeod and partly because he came to Ayr as a player-manager; it was known that he still possessed a high degree of skill and, at the age of thirty-four, it was a reasonable assumption that his skill had not eroded. A postponement at Clydebank on Monday, 27th December, was followed by another one on New Year's Day (Clyde at Douglas Park). This gave Mr Stainrod more time to get familiar with his new environs. On Hogmanay he announced that Malcolm Shotton would be his assistant manager while continuing to play for the club, and Sam McGivern would be the captain. He stated: "I don't want a captain who's just a yes man." As colleagues at Falkirk, Sam McGivern and Simon Stainrod had played as an attacking partnership. Malcolm Shotton said of his new role: "It's something I have wanted for a very long time and I'm delighted Simon has given me this opportunity."

Stainrod's career started at his local club, Sheffield United. He then went on to play for Oldham Athletic, Queen's Park Rangers, Sheffield Wednesday, Aston Villa, Stoke City, RC

Simon Stainrod with his trademark fedora.

Strasbourg, Rouen, Falkirk, Dundee and Leixoes. In 1982 he played for Queen's Park Rangers in the FA Cup final plus the replay which Spurs won 1-0. At Dundee he was initially a player then player-manager then director of football operations, a post he had quit earlier in season 1993/94 prior to playing in Portugal.

The cold snap released its grip sufficiently for the game at Clydebank to go ahead on 4th January, 1994. In the crowd of 2,152 the Ayr contingent was large and exuberant. Colin McGlashan and Greg Hood had the team 2-0 up by the thirteenth minute by which time we were all in a frenzy. The national media's interest in this game centred upon Davy Cooper's return to Clydebank but the show was stolen by Simon Stainrod who played for the last seven minutes. This was all the time he needed to exhibit that he was a natural footballer. The 2-0 win put Ayr United back into seventh place, just on the right side of the reconstruction cut-off. Getting drawn to play at Kilmarnock in the Scottish Cup offered a wealth of photo opportunities. Mr Stainrod's habitual headgear was a fedora and a lot of fans took to sporting it. Before a crowd of 12,856 the tie was lost 2-1 to a penalty kick - wrongly given, because Malcolm Shotton was proven to have made no contact with Shaun McSkimming.

In March 1994 Mr Stainrod announced that he was keen to bring Cantona to Ayr for a trial. Alas, it was Joel, the less illustrious of the Cantona brothers. Besides, he opted for Stockport County while his brother Eric continued with his legendary status at nearby Manchester United.

The evening of 29th March, 1994, was vital. Merely one point separated Ayr United from eighth-placed Stirling Albion. The seventh-placed relegation cut-off rendered it a four-pointer. Stirling Albion 1 Ayr United 3 was the happy outcome. Although stretching our safety buffer nine fixtures had yet to be played. After these were negotiated we remained seventh to guarantee a place in the second tier of what would now be four leagues rather than three. The conclusion of 1993/94 saw Ayr United

Franck Rolling.

placed nineteenth out of the thirty-eight Scottish league clubs (soon to be forty). Analysis of this statistic could simplistically draw the conclusion that the Ayr United of 1994 was average. Yet the word 'average' was not in Mr Stainrod's vocabulary. In the programme for the Ayr United versus St. Mirren match on 14th May, 1994, he wrote: "The days of Ayr United being an insignificant club are over."

The ever popular Malcolm Shotton left the club in July to take up a coaching role at Barnsley. Sam McGivern then became the assistant manager. The loss of Shotton at the heart of the defence was compensated for by the signing of Franck Rolling, a 25-year-old Frenchman whom Mr Stainrod had known from his time at Strasbourg. Other signings were made in order to pursue a policy of turning Somerset Park into "a land of giants." His thinking was that players with a large physique would create a more intimidating presence. Garry Paterson and Ian Gilzean both fell into that category. He knew them from his time at Dundee and persuaded them to sign for Ayr. John Sharples, latterly of Hearts and formerly of Manchester United, made the following comment when he signed: "It's a good club. Simon has a few decent players here and I think they could possibly be pushing in the league, or else I wouldn't have come. He's certainly got the place buzzing."

That last comment was most pertinent. Optimism was high. Sound bites were teeming in positivity and pre-season preparation in the Republic of Ireland was a most useful exercise in team bonding. Simon Stainrod kept saying that he wished his team to make persistent use of the long ball and aerial bombardments. In time he admitted it was a ruse and that he just wanted to feed the media with this story in order that opponents would expect a different type of approach from the one being used. It actually worked. On the night of 16th August, 1994, Celtic won 1-0 at Ayr in a League Cup tie. Their goal was scored in the second minute. Celtic boss Tommy Burns said in his post-match comments: "Every time Ayr launched the ball

Ian Gilzean.

into our box I was holding my breath to see if they would get a flick on or a deflection."

Contrary to expectation the league season descended into a struggle and only the even worse form of Stranraer kept the club off bottom place. Mr Stainrod was well-connected and he strove hard in pursuit of an improvement. In a 1-0 defeat away to St. Mirren on 5ᵗʰ November, 1994, a club record was set. It set a record for the most foreign players on the pitch for Ayr United at the same time. They were Niclas Nylen (Swedish), Claudio Valetta (Italian), Franck Rolling (French), Bruce Murray (American) and Regis Gorgues (French). One week later we had five again during the course of a 3-0 defeat at home to Airdrie. These comprised four from the previous game, Bruce Murray being the exception, but including Jose Fortes (Portuguese). A fortnight after that Franck Rolling was the only foreigner in the starting line-up for a 1-1 draw away to Dundee.

On the second Saturday of December a calamitous 6-0 defeat at Dunfermline had no redeeming features. Mr Stainrod was adept at positivity but even a politician could not have talked up what had happened. The response was to beat Premier League Kilmarnock 4-1 at Ayr a week later. Getting custody of the Ayrshire Cup helped to lift the mood yet there was no escaping the league table. At the midpoint of the league programme Ayr United sat second from the foot with two wins out of eighteen. Third bottom St. Mirren had four points more and had played a game less. With two going down automatically the situation was critical. It was soon to become even more critical. Losing 2-1 at home to Hamilton Accies on Hogmanay was compounded by Stranraer winning 3-2 at Clydebank. This meant that Ayr United and Stranraer were joint bottom with not only the same number of points but also an identical number of goals for and against. The teams were due to meet.

On 2ⁿᵈ January, 1995, there was chaos at Stranraer. In the 75ᵗʰ minute Lex Grant put the home side 2-0 ahead. This was the cue for Ayr fans to migrate from behind the goal in order to barrack Simon Stainrod and the Ayr United directors. The protesters even sang the name of Stranraer boss Alex McAnespie. It ended 2-0 and Simon Stainrod vowed to fight on.

Beating St. Mirren 2-0 at Ayr in the next match eased a little pressure and, on defeating Dundee 1-0 at Somerset Park on 11th February, the bottom two was escaped. After failing to win either of the next six league fixtures the club was plunged back into the bottom two and there was no recovery. Relegation with foot of the table Stranraer was Ayr United's lot.

On 26th August, 1995, Steve Archibald, player-manager of East Fife, lined up against Ayr United in a Second Division fixture (third tier) at Bayview Park. If Simon Stainrod had not been injured, it would have meant that they would have been in opposition to each other for the first time since the 1982 FA Cup final replay at Wembley. In contrast, the attendance here in 1995 was 743. The Ayr faction voiced dissent at losing 1-0. This was the second league fixture of the season, the opener having been more tolerable (Ayr United 1 Clyde 1). The East Fife defeat was so intolerable that the Ayr United Travel Club prepared a written statement to express "their disgust at the performance." It then went on to accuse Simon Stainrod of "living in Cloud Cuckoo land." The forthright statement also said: "We strongly advise that the manager leaves before the rest of our loyal hard core support does."

Ostensibly there was an early chance to atone. Berwick Rangers had not won at Ayr since 27th February, 1965, so there was little historical precedent for them winning here on 2nd September, 1995. Ayr United 1 Berwick Rangers 4 – the fans booed and jeered with all the vocal strength that could be mustered. On the Tuesday morning of 5th September he said that he would not be resigning. Less than three hours later his resignation was announced after a meeting with chairman Bill Barr. The *Ayrshire Post* headline on the Berwick report was **DISGRACE**.

In the aftermath of that last match the soon-to-be-departed manager said that his players "should get done by the Fraud Squad". He also denounced the supporters as moaners. That last point was hardly open to argument. The supporters were indeed moaners and the author was moaning as much, if not more, than anybody else. There was much to moan about. Of course there were times when his relationship with the fans was completely harmonious. A personal favourite Simon Stainrod incident happened on 6th May, 1995. In a 3-0 win at home to Stranraer he scored directly from a corner-kick then celebrated with a handspring.

He managed Ayr United in fifty-seven First Division matches and three in the Second Division. He won thirteen, a ratio of less than one in four. During his reign he used precisely fifty players in first team competitive action. His next job in football was as an agent.

Gordon Dalziel

September 1995 – November 2002

In the history of Ayr United the only manager to exceed Gordon Dalziel in respect of timespan and achievement has been Ally MacLeod. Yet he came to Ayr as a player with the proviso that he would also have a coaching role. On Friday 7th July, 1995, he was signed from Raith Rovers in a terrific coup. At Raith Rovers he became the club's highest scorer of all time. In the season recently finished Ayr United's top league scorer was Justin Jackson with a miserly total of four. The need for a proven scorer need hardly be explained. In 1994/95 Raith had won the League Cup and the First Division title. His transfer to Ayr came at a time when the club had just been relegated to the third tier and full-time contracts were gradually being phased out. The coaching involvement must have been an influential factor in his decision. In his career to this point he had been at Rangers, Manchester City, Partick Thistle, East Stirling then Raith Rovers.

After the demise at home to Berwick Rangers and the resultant departure of Simon Stainrod, Gordon Dalziel was placed in interim management. His first match was at home to Forfar Athletic and he claimed that he was more nervous before this match than he was before the previous season's League Cup final. Forfar had last won in the league at Ayr on 30th September, 1967, this comprising their only league win ever at Ayr to this point. This game in 1995 was lost 3-1. Gordon Dalziel scored in the match but missed the second half through

Ayr United versus Kilmarnock on 14th February, 1998. From left to right the players are Paul Wright (Kilmarnock), John Traynor, Keith Hogg and Kristjan Finnbogason.

injury. The club now sat second from the foot of the Second Division with one point from four games. Leaders East Fife had twelve points. One week later another longstanding sequence was broken with a 2-0 defeat at Stirling. It was Ayr United's first defeat at Stirling since 5th December, 1964. The statistical theme will be maintained to let you know that the next match was won 1-0 at Montrose. This was on 23rd September, 1995, yet it was Ayr United's first away league win since 16th April, 1994. Three weeks later Stenhousemuir won 2-1 at Ayr. It was their first win at Somerset Park since 20th April, 1963. A fortnight after that East Fife got their first league win at Ayr ever. On the day after that Stenhousemuir defeat the author had a meeting with chairman Bill Barr and his fellow directors. Mr Barr suggested the meeting in order to air my complaints about the direction of the club. It was clear that the infrastructure of the club was very sound, albeit that this was inconsistent with results. The managerial appointment was still under consideration via a wealth of applications. On Tuesday, 31st October, it was announced that Gordon Dalziel was the successful applicant and that Ally Dawson would be his assistant. In relation to the announcement he said: "I'm ready to pull this place apart." He was as good as his word. In a single season, 1995/96, Ayr United used forty-five players in competitive action. This was one more than the previous highest, from season 1917/18. The record of forty-five was beaten by one in 1997/98 as Mr Dalziel continued to work tirelessly.

In his first match in permanent charge Stirling Albion won 2-1 at Ayr. This was on 4th November but it transpired that this was our last home league defeat of the season. It was to take until 14th September, 1996, for an opposition club to next annexe full league points at Somerset Park. From mid-February 1996 he ceased to select himself in the starting line-up but by then the momentum was rolling. Finishing sixth was an acceptable achievement when considered against the failings of the opening months. The fans could see the recovery happening.

Mick Oliver with the Ayr United youth team in March 1997. This team reached the semi-finals of the BP Youth Cup.

This was evidenced by the fact that Ayr United had the highest average gate in the Second Division in 1995/96.

An early season League Cup win at Kilmarnock went down especially well with the fans. "Dalziel, there's only one Dalziel" was a song now getting sung with increasing regularity. A year to the weekend after losing 4-1 at home to Berwick Rangers, Ayr United won 6-0 against that club at Somerset Park, Berwick having already lost 5-0 here on 2nd March. Speculation linked him with the managerial vacancy at Raith Rovers. His response left no scope for ambiguity: "I'm staying here." He had not been approached by Raith anyway. Tommy McLean took the Raith job then switched to Dundee United after one match. When the vacancy emerged again he was approached but he said that he still wanted to stay at Ayr.

A 2-1 victory away to Queen of the South on 21st September was the first of seven consecutive league wins. By February 1997 Mr Dalziel was concerned about complacency. He need not have had any concerns. The league title was clinched with a 2-0 win away to Berwick Rangers on the final day although promotion had already been assured three weeks earlier. Merely one league defeat had been suffered in the last nineteen fixtures and the points total of seventy-seven remains a club record, although it should be acknowledged that past glories had occurred when two points, rather than three, were on offer for a win. Gordon Dalziel was a workaholic and he had reaped the fruits of his labour.

He demanded high standards. For example he was unhappy with the first half performance in a home match against Airdrie on 22nd November, 1997. The team had a 3-0 lead and it finished 6-0. Yet it was never in his nature to do anything that would upset the spirit of the team. He even took his squad to a Buddy Holly musical in Glasgow in order to lift morale ahead of a Scottish Cup visit from Kilmarnock on 14th February, 1998. Did this excursion have the desired effect? You can draw your own conclusion from the 2-0 win against the holders. Yet results

Goalkeeper David Castilla and Andy Millen.

elsewhere that afternoon conspired to drop Ayr United into second bottom place. With two clubs destined to go straight down this was perilous. By the last Saturday of the season it was even more perilous. At least a draw was required away to Partick Thistle in order to avoid relegation. Compounding the difficulty was the fact that the home team had to win to escape the drop. For the fifth consecutive week the players were taken to a top hotel forty-eight hours in advance. The preparations were thorough and the match was won 3-1.

Thirteen players were released at the end of the season. When it came to recruiting players Gordon Dalziel was excellent at selling the benefits of signing for Ayr United. In attempting to ward off the competition he even used to go so far as to promote Ayr as a nice place to live. In 1998/99 he was further successful in instilling a winning mentality. After winning 2-0 at Airdrie on 21ˢᵗ November, the club occupied top place in the First Division, ultimately finishing a creditable third behind Hibs and Falkirk. Glynn Hurst scored twenty goals in league and cup while Andy Walker scored nineteen. In the Scottish Cup Kilmarnock were beaten 3-0 at Ayr. It meant that Gordon Dalziel's Ayr United had knocked Kilmarnock out of cup competitions in three consecutive seasons. Had it not been for a late penalty miss at home to Dundee United he would have been only the second Ayr United manager ever to have taken the club to a Scottish Cup semi-final. However that accolade was merely deferred for a year. The club record for consecutive away league wins dates to 1958/59 with seven. There were six consecutive away league wins in 1998/99.

In the Scottish Cup run of 1999/2000 he guided the club past Premier League clubs Dundee and Motherwell then Second Division Partick Thistle on the way to a semi-final that was lost to Rangers. Only in 1973 had Ayr United previously reached this stage of the Scottish Cup and he would become our first manager to achieve this twice. The dramas in the cup were not replicated in the league. Merely seventh place was achieved.

Pat McGinlay.

Mr Dalziel was at his persuasive best in the summer of 2000. In attracting the quality of James Grady, Eddie Annand, John Hughes and Pat McGinlay, more was required than financial clout. These players had no shortage of suitors. The vision for the club had to be sold to them. Was that vision over embellished? No! In 2000/01 his team finished as runners-up. One year earlier Dunfermline Athletic had been granted promotion on attaining this position but in 2001 a mild restructuring meant that only champions Livingston went up. Not that Ayr United could have been promoted anyway. In early April the dictatorship known as the SPL stated that the club could not be promoted owing to the stadium criteria. By then the Heathfield application was gradually getting choked by red tape.

Nonetheless the boss could draw positives. 2000/01 saw the club's highest ever finish in the new-style First Division. There was only one home league defeat. In the last seventeen league fixtures just one loss was suffered. With seventy-three goals we were the highest scorers in the second tier. Five league defeats overall comprised the fewest of any club in the First Division. A highlight was beating third-place Falkirk 6-0. It was relevant too that Ayr United were the champions of the Scottish Professional Youth League.

Season 2001/02 was a very good endorsement of just how fickle football can be. On 10th November, 2001, Arbroath won 1-0 at Somerset Park. This result left Ayr United second bottom of the First Division. An improvement manifested itself to such a degree that a third-place finish would be achieved. However the allusion to fickleness is not a reference to the league revival. In the League Cup, Ayr United had already beaten Stranraer and Kilmarnock. The team then went on to knock out Inverness Caledonian Thistle then Hibs in a Hampden semi-final. For the first time in the history of the club an Ayr United team would be playing in a national final. Running alongside this success was a Scottish Cup run in which we

The championship trophy 1997.

knocked out Deveronvale, Dunfermline Athletic and Dundee United to reach the semi-finals. On 17th March, 2002, Gordon Dalziel became the first (and so far only) manager to lead an Ayr United team out at a national final. Alas the League Cup final was lost 4-0 to an expensively-assembled Rangers team. Six days later we were all back ay Hampden for a Scottish Cup semi-final against Celtic. The 3-0 margin of defeat was harsh. In the *Ayr Advertiser* report the injustice of the scoreline was alluded to: "Ayr were outstanding in all areas of the park and played probably some of the best football of Gordon Dalziel's reign." Two major matches in a matter of days yet the Arbroath defeat in November prompted a petition to get rid of the manager.

On 16th November, 2002, Ayr United beat St. Johnstone 2-0. It was the club's first win at McDiarmid Park. Our previous win in Perth had been in the final match played at Muirton Park prior to it being demolished. That match had taken place on 29th April, 1989. On the Wednesday evening of 20th November Mr Dalziel stepped down as manager but remained at the club as a coach. This happened on his own suggestion. The timing was peculiar. The team had just had its best result of the season so far.

During his time in charge it was almost taken for granted that his Ayr United team would overcome Premier League opponents in cup competitions. In the Scottish Cup such victims were Kilmarnock twice, Dundee, Motherwell, Dunfermline Athletic and Dundee United. In the League Cup his top-sphere victims were Kilmarnock twice, Motherwell and Hibs. The four-in-a-row against Kilmarnock held particular appeal for the fans. It seems appropriate too to repeat that no one else has managed the club to a national final and that he was in charge for two of the three Scottish Cup semi-finals contested by Ayr United. A criticism sometimes levelled at him is that he did not get the club into the Premier League. The counter argument is that there was formerly a time when second place in the second tier was enough for promotion regardless of stadium criteria.

After our home game against Ross County on 29th November in the following year, he left, his contract having expired. In June 2004 he got back into management with Glenafton Athletic and in October that year he moved back to Raith Rovers to take charge. In 2007 he made the reverse move, eventually quitting Glenafton Athletic in August 2009.

Campbell Money

November 2002 – August 2004

A clichéd football scenario involves a player joining a club then declaring that they have supported that club since they were a boy. Additional emphasis might come in the form of kissing the badge. When Campbell Money said that he supported Ayr United as a boy he was not trying to conform to one of those patronising stereotypes. He was a genuine fan. In his youth it was clear that he had a future as a goalkeeper. Inevitably he moved on from Dailly Amateurs to St. Mirren where he remained from 1978 until 1996. He was in the St. Mirren Scottish Cup winning team in 1987 and this was the only senior club he played for. On 6th August, 1991, his testimonial match took place. From 1996 he managed Stranraer where he won the League Challenge Cup in his first season. Then, in 1998, he saw his club win promotion to the second tier.

In May 1999 he left Stranraer to become the head of Ayr United's youth development. This was a full-time position and his success was tangible. His young players were the Scottish Professional Youth League champions for 2000/01 and then again in 2001/02. On 10th April, 2002, the team contested the Scottish Youth Cup final, losing 4-2 against their Rangers counterparts at Hamilton. The full coaching team was Campbell Money, Norrie McWhirter, Sammy Conn and George Logan. Three days later six teenagers were in the first team squad for a First Division fixture which was drawn 0-0 at home to Falkirk. On 27th July that year Stranraer won 4-2 at Ayr in a pre-season

Campbell Money.

friendly but the composition of the Ayr team was very young. With the ages in brackets that team was: Brian Hamilton (18), Willie Lyle (18), Michael Dunlop (19), Aaron Black (18), Martin Ferry (19), David Craig (33), Craig Bingham (22), Stewart Kean (19), Andrew Ferguson (17), Mark McColl (17) and Paul Sheerin (27); substitutes – Robert Burgess (17), Scott Chaplain (18), James Latta (17), Stuart McGrady (17), Steven Crawford (15) and Darren Johnson (16). David Craig limped off after eighteen minutes to be replaced by Robert Burgess and Paul Sheerin played the first half only. This meant that, in the second half, the oldest Ayr player was 22-year-old Craig Bingham.

When Gordon Dalziel stepped down as manager on the night of 20th November, Campbell Money became his successor with immediate effect. Upon his appointment he said: "I well remember coming to Somerset Park as a boy. The first game I saw was against Queen of the South in 1965 and I was in the record crowd when Ayr beat Rangers four years later."

His first game as the boss was a comfortable 3-1 home win against Alloa Athletic. He had extensive knowledge of the club's youth system and it was generally wondered whether he would implement that knowledge by promoting youngsters to the first team. We did not have to wonder for long. On 28th December, 2002, Ayr United beat Arbroath 4-0 in a league fixture at Somerset Park. Three of the Ayr scorers were teenagers (the other scorer was Mark Campbell). They were Stewart Kean (19 years 299 days), Mark McColl (two days after his 18th birthday) and Andrew Ferguson (17 years 279 days). Ferguson was not in the starting line-up (84th minute sub for McColl). Boyd Mullen (five days short of his 17th birthday) went on in the 85th minute for Scott Chaplain (19 years 80 days). The starting line-up also included Willie Lyle (18 years 258 days) and Marc Smyth who had only just ceased to be a teenager (it was the day after his 20th birthday). At the final whistle the fans drifted towards the exits while raving about the clinical performance they had just seen from a young team.

Mark Campbell.

An early endorsement of Mr Money's capabilities came in the shape of the Bells Division One Manager of The Month award for February 2003. The team went on to finish sixth while the Professional Youth League title was won for the third consecutive year.

In 2003/04 a relegation battle developed. Following a 1-1 draw at home to Queen of the South on 3rd January, 2004, John Connolly made an interesting observation. Connolly had made over a hundred first team appearances for Everton in his day and he had once been at the head of the Ayr United youth set-up. Here in 2004 he was the manager of Queen of the South. His comments were: "I sincerely hope that Ayr stay up and, if they continue to play like they did in the second half, they will. Campbell Money has got them going and if they can survive this season they will be a real threat next term." Notwithstanding the fight against the drop, the Ayr United board agreed with Mr Connolly's assessment. Later in the month Campbell Money agreed a deal to tie him to the club until 2006.

A 2-0 win at home to St. Mirren on 21st February lifted the club out of the bottom two. Before that match there was a minute's silence for Ally MacLeod and the general attitude was 'let's do it for Ally'. Of course the unforgiving world of professional football has little cognisance of sentiment and the club found its way back into the bottom two. On 13th March we had a six-pointer away to Raith Rovers whom we trailed by four points. Before the game there was a minute's silence for the victims of the Madrid train bombings. This was especially poignant in view of the Spanish players in the home squad. Raith Rovers won 2-1 to go seven points clear of Ayr United. We were now bottom, one point behind Brechin City. Mr Money had a dislike of making excuses. If he had been otherwise minded he would have had a glaring excuse on this particular day. Raith's equalising goal came from the most dubious of penalties. Ramon Pereira went down in the box on being challenged by Lee Hardy. He hit the proverbial deck on his own propulsion.

It was clearly a wrong decision. The Ayr United support vented fury in the time-honoured manner but our manager chose not to be critical of the decision in his post match interviews.

On 8th May a 0-0 draw away to Falkirk (at Ochilview Park) sealed relegation mathematically. One week later the completed First Division table showed Ayr United saved from the bottom by Brechin City only. The concept was simple – two down!

In June 2004 Norrie McWhirter was named as the assistant manager. The managerial pairing had been team mates at St. Mirren. This was not one of those 'old pals' appointments. McWhirter had been doing sterling work in relation to youth development at Somerset Park. Pre-season activity was hectic with the usual mix of agreeing deals with out-of-contract players and identifying affordable prospects. A July win at home to Kilmarnock brought custody of the West Sound Big Match Trophy but the effect on morale exceeded any thrill at seeing the trophy.

Losing 1-0 at Dumbarton in the opening league game was perceived to be a setback but nothing more. Three points got picked up at home to Berwick Rangers a week later and it seemed that the quest for promotion was back on track. League fixture number three was a 2-1 defeat at Stranraer yet it was far from a debacle. The home team's 83rd minute winner came from a burst of individual brilliance. David Graham started a run in his own half, evaded all challengers then rifled an exquisite drive beyond Ludovic Roy from outside the box. This turned out to be Campbell Money's last match as manager of Ayr United. Both he and Norrie McWhirter resigned. The timing seemed inexplicable. It was still August, besides which his contract was not due to expire until 2006.

He had future spells in management with Stenhousemuir and Cumnock Juniors. In June 2009 he accepted a post with the SFA. His role was that of Scottish Football Youth Initiative Development and Monitoring Co-ordinator. It was not the briefest of job titles but it clearly recognised that he was identified as a man who had a great skill for youth development.

Mark Shanks

August 2004 – March 2005

Campbell Money had been appointed with no undue deliberation and the same was true of his successor. Mark Shanks became the new manager on Friday, 27th August, 2004, just six days after Campbell Money's last match. His full managerial team was named with equal punctuality. Ex-Ayr United players Robert Connor and Robert Reilly were named as his assistants along with Jim Dempsey. Shanks, Reilly and Dempsey were all joining from Kilwinning Rangers.

In June 1979 Mr Shanks was signed for Ayr United as a right-back after being freed by Motherwell. Willie McLean was now signing him for the second time, having acquired his signature for Motherwell after his departure from Blackburn Rovers. Those of us of a certain vintage could recall his father playing for Airdrie. Mark Shanks won the Ayr United Supporters' Association Player of the Year award for 1980/81. What made this all the more remarkable was the fact that his fellow full-back was no less than Stevie Nicol. On Wednesday, 8th October, 1980, Mark Shanks had played in direct opposition to the illustrious George Best. It was a League Cup quarter-final tie in which Ayr United drew 2-2 with Hibs on the night. The *Glasgow Herald* report mentioned that George Best looked unhappy. Best did not play in the second leg, which Ayr United won 2-0.

After Mark Shanks' release, it was announced in June 1985 that he would be playing in Cyprus in the season ahead. Yet in November that year he made his debut for Dumbarton and from 1986 until 1990 he played for Queen of the South.

Mark Shanks – Ayr United Supporters' Association Player of The Year 1980/81.

In the world of football management he had experience with Cumnock Juniors, Queen of the South, Albion Rovers then Kilwinning Rangers.

On the day after taking up the Ayr job he sent out a team to face Morton at Somerset Park. A 2-0 win was the pleasing outcome. The club worst for consecutive games with a sending off is four. These were all league games and they spanned September to October 2004. The habitually disadvantaged Ayr team got three draws and a defeat during this spell of lax discipline. A win at Berwick was followed by a home defeat against Dumbarton in which another red card was picked up. Finishing with ten men in five games out of six was in contrast to the fact that thus far in the season only one player had been sent off in opposition to Ayr United. That player was Brechin City's Kevin McLeish who had gone on as a substitute at Ayr in stoppage time only to be sent back off fifteen seconds later.

Progress was proving difficult. A 5-0 defeat at Brechin was followed by the sale of Stewart Kean to St. Mirren. When 2004 gave way to 2005 there was little in the way of respite. On 3rd January, Mark Shanks tasted victory over Morton for the third time in the season, but in mid-month there was a 5-1 demise at Alloa. The optimists amongst us continued to ponder the vague possibility of promotion. On 26th February we were dealt a dose of realism when bottom club Berwick Rangers won at Ayr. We were now thirteen points behind second-placed Stranraer. On Tuesday, 1st March, Mr Shanks quit his job but did not state his reasons. He informed the full-time players before that morning's training session.

In May 2005 he was named as the manager of Troon Juniors with Jim Dempsey becoming a coach there. It was described as a "temporary management team". During the following month Dempsey was installed as manager there. In November 2006 Mark Shanks became the manager of Cumnock Juniors. He was ultimately replaced by Campbell Money at Cumnock, the man he had replaced at Ayr.

Mr Shanks returned to Somerset Park as the Head of Youth Development. He stepped down from that role in September 2009.

Robert Connor

March 2005 – February 2007

The history of Ayr United contains the names of many great full-backs. Robert Connor is one of them. In midfield he was equally proficient. In the summer of 1977 he was called up from Ayr United Boys' Club and he made his first team debut on 15th March, 1978. On that evening he was in the starting line-up for a Premier League fixture at home to Partick Thistle. The old saying about 'the calm before the storm' was reversed. It kicked-off with a sleet storm in progress, then he went on to put in a composed performance. By the end of the season he could number nine league starts.

It was potentially daunting for a seventeen-year-old to be stepping into a team fighting against relegation, especially since it was a losing battle. John Murphy was in his last season at the club and he had already worn the number three shirt in that campaign. He predicted that Robert Connor would play for Scotland one day and he was right. Of course Spud was eminently qualified to know a good left-back. He had been playing for Ayr United in that position since 1963 and he remains unsurpassed for the number of appearances by any player at the club.

On 17th March, 1980, Robert Connor was an unused substitute for the Scottish League versus the League of Ireland in Dublin but his club mate Eric Morris played the entire match. Then, in June, a Scotland semi-professional team won a four-nation tournament in Holland. A 3-0 win over Holland was followed

Robert Connor.

by a 4-2 win over England. A draw was needed against Italy in the final match and it ended 0-0. In the win over England all of the goals were scored by Ayr United players. The scorers were Robert Connor with two and one each from Eric Morris and Gerry Christie.

On the evening of 8th September, 1981, the Scotland under-21 team beat their Swedish counterparts 4-0 at Easter Road. The Scotland full-backs comprised the Ayr United pairing of Nicol and Connor. In 1983 and again in 1984 there were last-day escapes when the club was faced with relegation to the third tier. Robert Connor had lodged a transfer request as far back as October 1982 but his transfer did not materialise until the summer of 1984 when he was sold to Dundee for £50,000 by which time his regular position was in midfield. On 29th April, 1986, he made his full Scotland debut against Holland. He made three more Scotland appearances all of which were after his move to Aberdeen. His next club was Kilmarnock and he returned to Ayr United for 1996/97, a Second Division championship winning season. On 13th August, 1996, he scored the only goal of the tie when Ayr United won at Kilmarnock in the League Cup yet in his two seasons with Kilmarnock he did not score at all. After his season back at Ayr his next club was Partick Thistle, followed by Queen of the South.

In August 2004 he rejoined Ayr United as a coach. On Friday, 4th March, 2005, the board issued a statement to the effect that Robert Connor would be the interim manager with Robert Reilly as his assistant. On the same day Robert Connor was interviewed on Radio Scotland and the interviewer referred to Ayr United being managed by the two Bobs, before cheekily saying that two bob was the value of the club! The next day was the occasion of a 1-1 draw at home to Alloa Athletic. There was another battle running parallel to the battle for league points. The club was having to combat apathy. On the night of 15th March losing 1-0 to Brechin City was bad enough but the attendance of 742 was alarming. It was the lowest attendance for a competitive match at Somerset Park since 17th March, 1984, when 673 attended an Alloa match, that being the lowest crowd at the ground for a competitive match since 1965.

On Monday, 2nd May, it was confirmed that Robert Connor had been appointed as manager rather than just interim manager. Robert Reilly's appointment as his assistant was also confirmed. Mr Connor commented: "We have a playing squad of thirty and the majority will be released." That weekend the season stumbled to a close with a 1-1 draw at home to Dumbarton. Eighth out of ten was a disappointing finish in the third tier. One win out of the last twelve matches was a grave concern. Thirty-six goals scored was the worst record in that league, bottom club Berwick Rangers even managing one more. Yet having been in the job since March, Mr Connor had not had the benefit of a pre-season in which to build.

The building job referred to was rendered all the more difficult with the loss of Ludovic Roy, Andrew Ferguson, Paddy Connolly and Marc Smyth. More positively a plan was initiated in order to nurture a new generation of Ayr United players. A not-for-profit-company was launched to take over the running costs of the club's youth and community development programme. The independent body Ayr United Football Academy Limited was set up with five people. They were John Dalton, Tom Young, Robert Gardiner, Alan McGregor and Graham Hough. Eric Morris was soon appointed as the head youth coach. His remit was to oversee the development of the football academy. This was a brilliant initiative but in the immediate term Robert Connor had to raid the junior market to acquire Chris Strain (Troon Juniors), Ian Cashmore (Kilwinning Rangers), Martyn Campbell (Irvine Meadow), Raymond Logan (Pollok Juniors), Paul Hyslop (Auchinleck Talbot), Chris Robertson (Hurlford United), Martyn Campbell (Irvine Meadow), Eric Phillips (Auchinleck Talbot) and Andy Essler (Maryhill Juniors).

The new recruits acquitted themselves well in the early season. Beating First Division Ross County at Dingwall in the

League Cup in midweek was followed by a 2-2 league draw at Gretna on the Saturday. A week before the Gretna match we had drawn 1-1 at home to Peterhead in what was our first ever league match against that club. We had never played Gretna in the league before either, but we went there in the knowledge that the home club had won all of their previous twenty-two league fixtures at Raydale Park. Breaking the sequence was an achievement in itself. A 1-0 reverse at home to Morton on 24th September was the club's first league defeat of the season. It meant dropping to fourth place. This was the minimum requirement for an end-of-season play-off place.

Wiining 4-0 away to Morton on 25th March, 2006, was a quite staggering result against the second-placed club (top place being unachievable to all except the dominant Gretna). However we had just gone thirteen games without a win (eleven in the league, two in the Scottish Cup). It was also a late date for the first win of 2006. Finishing sixth at least staved off a threat of relegation that looked too real until late March.

That summer it was made known that Ayr United would not have a reserve team playing competitively in the season ahead. This decision was reached with the proviso that friendlies would be arranged to give game time to fringe players.

On June 27th Robert Connor was one member of an Ayr United party that flew out to California. Directors Lachlan Cameron and Lewis Grant travelled as did players Gareth Wardlaw, Paul Weaver, James McKinstry and David Lowing. The purpose of the trip was to study a coaching regime with the acronym CATZ (competitive athlete training zone). It was a regime designed to enhance the performance of athletes while reducing the risk of injury. This was innovative thinking although it prompted the question of whether it would be reflected in results.

A 2-0 win at Brechin on 23rd September, 2006, left Ayr United with thirteen points, every one of which had been gained away from home. In the next match Raith Rovers were beaten at Ayr to push the club into third position on the same points total as second-placed Stirling Albion. Morton remained top.

Mr Connor's favoured formation was 4:5:1. For the visit of Forfar Athletic on 28th October he instead opted for 4:4:2. The match was won 5-0. It was our biggest league win since 6th March, 2001, when Falkirk got annihilated 6-0 at Ayr. Such glories were to be savoured. 2006 ended with six consecutive league defeats. Losing 2-0 at home to Cowdenbeath on 24th February, 2007, bore depressing statistical analysis. The last fourteen league fixtures, including this one, had yielded just one Ayr United win. That solitary success had been the result of a stoppage time winner against Stranraer. The Cowdenbeath match was the proverbial straw that broke the camel's back.

Robert Connor, one of our greatest players of all time, was the subject of verbal abuse from the fans in his capacity as manager. His nickname was Roger. It was now a case of 'Roger and out'! Both he and his assistant Robert Reilly quit on the Monday.

Brian Reid, with Mark McGeown and Alex Ingram

March 2007

Robert Connor quit as manager on 26th February, 2007, and pending the appointment of Neil Watt, a temporary management team was put in place for three matches. That team comprised players Mark McGeown and Brian Reid as well as club director and former Ayr United striker Alex Ingram. Although a temporary arrangement there was pressure to get results. The first game under this set-up was at Stranraer who were in second bottom place and two points behind Ayr United with a game in hand. Defeat would have meant dropping into the Second Division relegation play-off position. Why worry? The match was won 3-0. Thereafter the three-part management team established a 100% record by defeating Forfar Athletic then Alloa Athletic, both games being at Ayr. Absolved of management responsibilities Brian Reid saw the season through in a playing role. Then he announced his retiral as a player.

Neil Watt

March 2007 – October 2007

An interesting football trivia question would be which Ayr United manager was born in Germany? You will have surmised from the heading that the answer is Neil Watt. His playing career encompassed Celtic, Forfar Athletic, East Stirling, Stirling Albion and Stranraer. On 8th December, 1984, he went on as a substitute for Stirling Albion in a Scottish Cup tie at home to Selkirk. In a scarcely credible 20-0 win he scored goals eighteen and nineteen.

On Thursday, 22nd March, 2007, he accepted the job of managing Ayr United. The news was well received. At this phase of history the name Neil Watt was persistently heard whenever Ayr United supporters speculated on the subject of who would be the best manager at the club. Yet such conversations took place more in hope than anything else. It was commonly considered that Mr Watt would not consider coming to Ayr. This was based on his decision to turn down the Dundee job when he was managing Stranraer. In April 2006 he quit Stranraer and, until taking the Ayr job, he had been out of football. He was now aged forty-four and was at Ayr on a part-time basis. This was due to him being a partner in the Glasgow-based factoring firm Hacking and Paterson. His assistant was named as Stuart Millar, who had worked alongside him at Stranraer.

The first match under Mr Watt's managership was a 2-2 draw at Peterhead which had required a stoppage time equaliser. In his post match comments he said: "As far as the play-offs go they are a long shot. We would have to win our last five games and hope that the teams above us lose most of theirs and that is unlikely." The reality proved that it was indeed unlikely but there was some late season cheer at Somerset Park, when an 86th minute goal from Ryan Stevenson beat champions Morton in the final league game. Few pondered too long on finishing fifth. We were now facing a third season in the Second Division. This was intolerably long. A promotion push was not just hoped for. It was expected.

During the 2007 close season a disproportionate amount of Mr Watt's signing activity was in respect of players with Stranraer on their CV. These players were David Hamilton, Michael Moore, Barry John Corr, Murray Henderson, Stephen Swift and Craig Higgins. There was a certain merit in recruiting players he had previously worked with, but the season developed in a way that was contrary to the pre-season expectation. On 20th October, Ross County had a 4-0 lead at Ayr by the 31st minute. It remained that way at the interval and this was somewhat embarrassing because Ayr United greats Sam McMillan, John Murphy and Henry Templeton conducted the half-time draw. The shouts of 'get yer bits oan' were inevitable.

Goalkeeper Barry John Corr did not reappear for the second half and he was released from his contract on 5th November without having returned to the club. The eventual damage against Ross County was restricted to 4-1. On the Monday, Neil Watt and Stuart Millar both quit.

In July 2009 Mr Watt became director of football with Clyde.

Brian Reid

October 2007 – May 2012

Brian Reid was a centre-half during his playing career. In turn his clubs were Morton, Rangers, Newcastle United, Morton again, Burnley, Dunfermline Athletic, Blackpool, Falkirk then Queen of the South. His next club was Ayr United. After signing on Tuesday, 12th September, 2006, he went straight into the starting line-up that night. His debut was in a Challenge Cup quarter-final against Clyde at Broadwood Stadium. Clyde won 1-0. This was our first away defeat in a competitive match since 18th February that year.

On Tuesday, 23rd October, 2007, he was named as the Ayr United manager. This was the day after Neil Watt resigned. Precisely three weeks afterwards Alistair Woodburn became the club's first signing from the Youth Academy. This bode well for the future but a 4-1 defeat at home to Cowdenbeath at the start of December caused Mr Reid to state categorically that he would be entering the transfer market in the January window. Three days later Scott MacKenzie was named as his assistant. As a player he had been with Falkirk, St. Mirren, Hamilton Accies and Queen of the South and his most recent job in football was as a youth coach at Dumbarton.

The *Ayrshire Post* was scathing in its condemnation of a 3-0 defeat at home to Raith Rovers in mid-December: "Those not fit to wear the once proud shirts must be shown the door". Note the emphatic 'must be' rather than 'should be'. A 2-0 defeat at Cowdenbeath three weeks later caused the *Ayrshire Post* to

Brian Reid.

replenish the stock of candid comments: "Gutless, spineless and clueless. After the false dawn of their New Year win over Berwick, Ayr United are back to their wretched worse."

From being second bottom at close of play on 9th February, 2008, the team went eight points clear of third bottom Queen's Park with a Tuesday night victory over Ross County on 11th March. Beating the league leaders 4-2 on their own ground was Brian Reid's best result in management to date. It was 4-0 at one stage. In the next midweek a 2-0 win was recorded at Airdrie and they were the second-placed club. Brian Reid won the Irn Bru Manager of the Month divisional award for March. A 3-1 win over Queen's Park in April was the sixth away league win out of seven. This was tantalisingly close to the club record of seven consecutive away league wins in 1958/59. It was too late to stave off a better league finish than seventh.

That summer Mr Reid busily prepared a squad for what would be a real promotion challenge. 2007/08 had been chequered but he had not had the advantage of a pre-season. In 2008/09 he could now be more accurately judged on his real capability. The result of the opening league game was already written in the statistics – Ayr United 0 Raith Rovers 0. It was the third time in our history that an opening league game was scoreless at home. Each time the gap was forty-two years (1924, 1966 and now 2008). Brian Reid won the Irn Bru Manager of the Month for August. He won the November award too and would win it again in March. On 21st February, 2009, Brechin City were beaten 4-2 at Ayr. After the matches played on that day we were three points behind leaders Raith Rovers with a game in hand. A midweek draw at home to Queen's Park on 4th March put Ayr United on top again but Brian Reid had to voice his dissatisfaction at half-time when the team was a goal down. Having beaten Queen's Park 3-0 at Hampden on the Saturday, victory had been expected.

A 5-0 win at home to Stranraer then preceded victory in a six-pointer away to Raith Rovers. Mr Reid was rightly positive but cautious in his post match comments: "It's a big, big win for us with another clean sheet but the league is not won or lost today – it's over the season. We are fortunate that we have four good strikers and when Mark Roberts and Bryan Prunty started to tire, I was able to freshen things up. David Gormley came on and chased a lost cause with a great finish for the winner." Top place was maintained until losing 1-0 at Brechin. With three games left Raith Rovers now had a two-point lead. On the expiry of the league programme the gap was the same.

In the play-offs Brechin City and Airdrie United were beaten on aggregate to secure the second promotion place. It transpired that Airdrie got promoted anyway because of Livingston's relegation to the Third Division due to financial misdealing. 2008/09 remains just one of five seasons in which Ayr United have been unbeaten at home in the league.

The club had been operating on a semi-full-time basis for several months. It had been done with some first team players joining youngsters and coaches from the Youth Academy for sessions on Tuesday and Thursday mornings. In reference to the proposal to expand the scheme the boss, who was now being rewarded with a full-time deal, said: "We have part-time players with jobs and can't ask them to give them up to go full-time. We will still be a predominantly part-time club but we will have some players in during the week. Players I target will have the option of signing part-time or full-time deals."

Part of the pre-season training took place in the Austrian town of Bischofshofen. While there German club Wacker Burghausen were beaten 3-0. In a friendly at Somerset Park, Unirea Urziceni won 2-1 with an own goal scored late in the match. It was a good showing against the Romanian champions, who were preparing for the Champions League. Entering October we sat seventh in the First Division table. In order we were above Dunfermline Athletic, Morton and Airdrie United. At the end of that month we were at the foot.

Survival was the minimum requirement but the likelihood gradually diminished with some degenerating late season form. 29th April, 2010, was an especially black day. Inverness Caledonian Thistle won 7-0 at Ayr. Assistant manager Scott MacKenzie commented: "I am speechless. I can't believe what I have just seen out there." None of us could! 1st May, 2010 – May day! How appropriate with Ayr United in such distress. With one game left these were the potential scenarios.

• Beat Morton at Cappielow by a three-goal margin to finish eighth and avoid relegation.
• Beat Morton by a one-goal or two-goal margin to finish ninth (play-off place) provided Airdrie United lose to Dunfermline Athletic.
• Neither of the above and straight relegation as the bottom club.

Airdrie United did lose but Ayr United lost 2-1. Eight defeats were suffered in the last nine league fixtures. Relegation coincided with the club's centenary year.

A 1-0 win at Alloa on 15th January, 2011, put Ayr United on top of the Second Division. To this point of the season Brian Reid had issued sporadic but justified criticism of his team. With things appearing to come right he and the fans were delighted. After that win he said: "Before the game I was thinking about our last trip here when we lost 4-1 but today things all ended well for us. I am pleased to win and go top of the table in what has been a great week for us." Within days it got even better. On the Tuesday night a Mark Roberts goal sufficed to beat Hibs in a Scottish Cup replay at Somerset Park. The club had a history of Scottish Cup wins against clubs from a higher division but Brian Reid was unique in being the only Ayr United manager to achieve it against a club from two divisions higher. In contrast the glory in the league began to fade. Adverse results, combined with the resurgent form of Livingston, still allowed runners-up status but the final gap at the top was twenty-three points. Thus began the play-off route which had proven successful two years earlier. After eliminating Forfar Athletic on aggregate then drawing in the first leg of the play-off final, the fans descended on Brechin City's Glebe Park in big numbers. An 88th minute winner from Michael Moffat generated great delirium and Ayr United were back in the second tier. Brian Reid was proving adept at winning promotion.

2011/12 was entered with thoughts of consolidating in the First Division or, at least, survival. An exciting distraction was the League Cup competition. A 3-0 win away to East Stirling caused nothing more than a ripple but the glory was compounded at each successful round. Inverness Caledonian Thistle were beaten 1-0 and, to a degree, it was a payback for their merciless 7-0 win on their previous visit to Ayr. Hearts were the next victims. They went home beaten in a shootout. In this particular season only Ayr United and Spurs conquered Hearts in cup competition. In the quarter-finals a late Chris Smith goal was enough to beat St. Mirren on their own ground. That made it the third conquest of a Premier League club and a fourth awaited in the semi-finals. Brian Reid's tactical awareness shone through in the St. Mirren win. He said: "We set out our shape and it worked a treat. We came more into it, caused them problems and had the best of the second half. We worked our socks off and deserved it."

The semi-final was contested against Kilmarnock at Hampden on 28th January, 2012. It was the first time the clubs had met at this venue and the attendance of 25,057 was the second highest ever for an Ayrshire derby. The only goal was scored by Kilmarnock in the nineteenth minute of extra time. Mr Reid commented: "Football can be so cruel and to lose the game to a stramash is so disappointing. I could see penalties looming and I fancied our chances with the form of Cuthbert and the fact we have some good takers. We deserved a clean sheet and I am really sorry that we couldn't send our magnificent supporters home happier." His defensive strategy was criticised but his game plan was nonetheless justified by the argument that it had been successful in eliminating St. Mirren. In the Scottish Cup the quarter-finals were reached at which staged Hibs avenged their defeat at Ayr the season before by winning 2-0. Parallel to these cup runs the league form was consistent enough to suggest that relegation would be averted. With Queen of the South getting cut adrift at the foot a play-off was shaping up to be the worst conceivable fate. In the closing weeks Raith Rovers made up ground and the feared play-off scenario materialised.

In the play-off semi-finals a scoreless draw at Airdrie was pleasing. The second leg was far from pleasing since we had two red cards, a 3-1 defeat and, as a consequence, relegation. Brian Reid quit on the Tuesday. Managers are popular or unpopular dependent on whether or not they succeed. Mr Reid's chequered managerial career at Ayr brought two promotions and two relegations. How the fans remember him is all down to whether you put the focus on the relegations or the promotions. Yet he remains one of the few Ayr United managers to get the club to a national semi-final and his time in charge brought cup wins over four Premier League clubs – Hibs, Inverness Caledonian Thistle, Hearts and St. Mirren.

In January, 2013, he became the manager of Global FC, a club in the Philippines. His next job in football was managing Nuneaton Town where his tenure lasted from April 2014 until September that year. He was then employed as a coach with Coventry City. Between May 2015 and January 2017 he was the manager of Stranraer.

Mark Roberts

May 2012 – December 2014

Brian Reid quit on Tuesday, 15th May, 2012, and Mark Roberts was named as his successor straight away. From signing for Ayr United from Partick Thistle on 30th January, 2009, until being appointed the manager's job he had scored fifty-four goals for Ayr United. He oozed enthusiasm and always gave off an impression that he simply loved playing football. Players with a Kilmarnock connection find it a bit more difficult to get accepted by the Ayr United support but Mark Roberts made that transition and even attained the captain's armband in the process. Particular highlights were the winning goal to knock Hibs out of the Scottish Cup the year before (he wrong-footed an entire line of defenders) and his equaliser in the play-off final at Brechin in the same year. He was a player who could produce the goods with a smile on his face. Not too many players would tell you that they loved taking penalties but Mark Roberts would openly tell people that he did enjoy taking them. In season 2010/11 he scored fourteen penalties out of the sixteen he took for Ayr United. On 18th September, 2010, he created a club record by scoring a hat-trick of penalties in a 3-2 win away to East Fife. The winner came in stoppage time.

His step into management was on a full-time basis. David White, head of youth at the club, was named as his assistant, also on a full-time basis.

Mr Roberts was released from Partick Thistle in the January 2009 transfer window and signed for Ayr United on the day

When reflecting on the play-off final at Brechin on 22nd May, 2011, Mark Roberts recounted a tale of being accidentally "taken out" by a fan when he wheeled away in celebration. Here is the evidence. Michael Moffat is helping him to his feet. Jonathan Tiffoney is to their right.

before the deadline was due to expire. Brian Reid named him in the starting line-up at home to Raith Rovers on the Saturday. Before Partick Thistle his clubs had been Kilmarnock, Raith Rovers (loan), Falkirk, Airdrie, Shelbourne, St. Mirren and Airdrie United. Little time expired before reports were punctuated with descriptions of his brilliant goals. "Mark Roberts turned and executed a brilliant volley from eighteen yards to make it 3-2" – Brechin City (home); "Mark Roberts scored with a cool finish" – also Brechin City (home); "Mark Roberts sent a sensational 18-yard drive into the top corner of the net" – Queen's Park (away).

By the summer of 2012 his predatory instincts had not deserted him but with the extra responsibility of management he seldom selected himself in the starting line-up. Thirty-five starts in 2011/12 shrunk to eight in 2012/13.

In May 2012 the new management duo had a seven-day summit with club owner Lachlan Cameron in California. Lachlan said: "Mark and Davy are both on the same page as me when it comes to how we develop the squad. There's no point in having a youth academy if we don't use it. The days of taking eighteen and nineteen-year-olds from other clubs are over."

Motherwell were beaten 4-0 in a pre-season friendly at Ayr. The visitors had finished third in the previous season's Premier League and were preparing for the qualifying rounds of the Champions League. Goalkeeper Darren Randolph conceded three of the goals; he was destined to play in the Premiership with West Ham United. Admittedly it had to be put into the perspective of a friendly but the display of attacking football was outstanding.

Four days later we had a 1-1 draw at home to Bolton Wanderers who had just dropped out of the Premiership. In the first round of the League Cup, Clyde were beaten 6-1 at Ayr despite the tie being scoreless at half-time. The attacking abandon in that second half was exhilarating to watch.

There was no reason to doubt that such form would be carried over into the league programme. The reality was one point from the first five fixtures. The status as the bottom club in the Second Division provoked the fury of the supporters.

In mid-December a 2-0 lead was surrendered to allow East Fife to win 3-2 at Somerset Park. After the match the boss said: "Although I'm angry with the result there are plenty of positives to take from the game, particularly the way we created chances. I honestly think the first forty-five minutes was about the best performance I've seen here for a long time. We could have scored ten goals and that's not an exaggeration."

His last point actually was an exaggeration but with the next match being against foot-of-the-table Albion Rovers it was at least expected that the run of three consecutive defeats would he halted. Alas not! It was Albion Rovers 2 Ayr United 0 and there was little in the way of festive spirit from the fans. The anger was justified. Mark Roberts commented: "I know the fans are frustrated but I can guarantee I'm more frustrated than them. It's my livelihood that's on the line. If things don't improve it could be curtains for me. These guys will go on websites and forums and say what they like but I've got to come back, get these players on top of their game and get out of this position."

Queen of the South were our First Foots on 2nd January, 2013, but they were very inhospitable guests, winning 5-1. It was our heaviest defeat at the start of a year since losing 4-0 away to Hamilton Accies on 2nd January, 1990.

After the Albion Rovers defeat Mark Roberts had said that his door was open to any fans who wished to discuss anything with him. The author took him up on that offer in early January. We sat in his office and it was clear from what he said that he was thoroughly committed to putting matters right. He came across as being passionate and dedicated but seemed to be at a loss to understand why his team had a flair for dropping out of matches after being dominant. 2012/13 was the season of the curse of the 2-0 lead, owing to a consistency in failing to win matches after attaining this scoreline.

The season finally ended with a 2-1 defeat at Forfar. It was our eighteenth consecutive game without a clean sheet. In finishing seventh in the Second Division we were fifty-one points behind champions Queen of the South. The pre-season and early season form had conspired to create the falsest of false dawns.

Quite naturally there was always going to be an element of caution when 2013/14 got underway. One positive aspect was Alan Forrest scoring a last minute winner against Queen's Park at Hampden in the Challenge Cup. He was aged 16 years 321 days, thereby making him the club's youngest ever scorer of a competitive goal.

A fortnight later we won 3-0 at Arbroath. This was the club's biggest away win in an opening league fixture since 1921 (Queen's Park 1 Ayr United 6) and our second biggest away opening league win ever.

Your writer further gloried in statistical glee when Mark Roberts scored in a 1-1 draw away to Stenhousemuir on 14th September, 2013. At 37 years 320 days this made him Ayr United's second oldest scorer of all time, the record being held by Darren Henderson (38 years 88 days when scoring against Stranraer on 8th January, 2005).

Losing 5-1 at Dunfermline a fortnight later was a crushing blow but fourth place was still maintained. In truth a play-off place was as much as could be achieved because Rangers were in the third tier at this time. With regular home attendances comfortably in excess of 40,000 their resources were comparatively vast. Even with a more conventional club at the top, the title would have been well beyond the grasp of Mark Roberts anyway.

Losing 6-3 at home to Stranraer on the evening of 12th November was a shocker of a result. The return at Stranraer on 4th January, 2014, was similarly horrific. 4-0 was the club's second highest defeat at Stair Park ever. At this point of history there had only ever been eleven instances of Ayr United starting a calendar year with a defeat of four goals or more. 2013 and 2014 was the only instance of it happening consecutively. In his post-match comments Mr Roberts made it clear that he was aware of the prevailing mood: "You've got to be thick-skinned as a manager, but I find it very disappointing that some of our support, who are the most knee-jerk by a mile, want me out." His comment about the support was in contrast to a remark Gordon Dalziel once made on the radio: "Ayr United supporters are highly demanding and rightly so."

There were fleeting glimmers of hope. After Airdrie had been beaten 3-0 at Ayr, Mr Roberts said: "Not many teams want to play against a strike force of Kyle and Moffat. Forrest is our spark. Every time he comes on he does well for us. Now I've a decision to make whether to start him next week because he does better when he comes off the bench."

Five days after the Airdrie win Michael Moffat was issued with a six-match ban for breaching the Scottish Football Association's rule 33 which concerned gambling.

Consecutive March Saturdays brought consecutive 5-0 wins against Stranraer (home) and East Fife (away). The only historical precedent for Ayr United winning 5-0 consecutively dated back to 24th February, 1979 (Montrose at home), and 28th February, 1979 (Clyde away). Before the Stranraer game Ayr United's goal difference was minus ten. It was now eliminated.

At the end of a largely uncomfortable season there was the considerable consolation that fourth place was enough for inclusion in the play-off semi-finals where we had to play Cowdenbeath. Our opponents were unlucky in having to get involved in the play-offs. In the last league game of the season they drew 1-1 at home to Queen of the South with the visitors equalising in the fifth minute of stoppage time. The consequence was that the Fifers rather than Alloa Athletic had to get involved in a scrap to avoid relegation.

Cowdenbeath won 2-1 at Ayr in the first leg and, although the chance of progressing was still alive, the visitors were visibly slicker and pacier. For the second leg the travelling fans outnumbered the home support but some were not even in the ground when Greg Stewart put the home team ahead nine seconds after the kick-off. This was a club record for the fastest goal conceded. It shaved one second off George Mulhall's goal for Aberdeen at Somerset Park on 20th October, 1956. Cowdenbeath went on to win 3-1 on the day and 5-2 on aggregate. This went down very badly with the fans and Mark Roberts was the main target for the wrath.

The response of chairman Lachlan Cameron was commendably blunt. He made it plain that relegation, or a sustained period in the wrong half of the table, would see Mark Roberts' contract terminated. He conceded that Mr Roberts was a young and first-time manager, and that he was backing him to learn from the experience. Mr Cameron's statement read:

"He succeeded in achieving the desired play-off position and, although there were definitely results that were horrendous along the way, he reached the target laid out for him. There is a section of our support who may not agree that keeping Mark for next year is acceptable but, as far as I am concerned, he reached the target and deserves the chance to improve on that. That, along with my belief that he is the right man for the job, is why his contract was renewed for the upcoming season. Too often football managers are cast away before they have a chance to flourish. It's a tough gig and it isn't made any easier by the current environment that allows clubs to overspend beyond their means and risk the future of our existence in doing so."

Mr Cameron then laid out five targets for Mark Roberts.

- Win League One or promotion through the play-offs.
- No relegation or bottom half run.
- Utilise and develop youth from the Academy.
- Ensure high level of discipline for himself and staff.
- Provide entertainment to the support.

The first three league matches of season 2014/15 were won. This was the first time Ayr United had done this since 1991/92 (when the first four were won). Top of the league after three games!

Was it another false dawn? Yes, it was! After some faltering form a win at Brechin on 20th September was enough to reclaim top spot. On 13th December, Stenhousemuir had a 3-2 win at Ayr. With one win out of the last eleven, including this one, it was now critical, all the more so because we were now second bottom. That figure of eleven included the Scottish Cup but excluded a match in which Peterhead had won at Ayr but had since been declared void.

After the Stenhousemuir defeat it was seventy minutes before he emerged from the dressing room. On the Monday evening he was dismissed and his parting comments were: "In twenty-three years in the game the day we won promotion at Brechin was the best I've ever had. I won leagues, cups, played in the Premier League and in Europe but Brechin, with its three pitch invasions, was my highlight. I will have that memory until I die."

How do Ayr United supporters recollect his Ayr United career? Are we more inclined to recall his track record as a player or as a manager? Whatever your opinion it has to be agreed that his final comments were superb. His next club was Clyde where he played and coached. On leaving Clyde he joined Hurlford United as a player.

Andy Millen

December 2014 – January 2015

Andy Millen made his Ayr United debut on 4th October, 1997, the occasion of a 2-1 home win over Stirling Albion. A fortnight earlier he had played for Raith Rovers at Ayr but he had since been purchased from that club for £30,000. Before Raith Rovers he had played for Pollok Juniors, St. Johnstone, Alloa Athletic, Hamilton Accies, Kilmarnock then Hibs.

His second match for Ayr United was a 1-1 draw away to St. Mirren in which he roamed upfield to equalise with a header in the 84th minute. He was ecstatic. After running behind the goal he almost finished in amongst the travelling support.

He lived up to his reputation as a combative defender right up until May 1999 when he joined Morton under freedom of contract. It was a surprise move since he had just captained Ayr United to third place in the First Division, Morton finishing sixth. He also had memories of knocking Kilmarnock out of the Scottish Cup in each of his two seasons.

His next club after Morton was Clyde whom he left in December 2003 to become the assistant manager of St. Mirren while still retaining a playing connection. On 15th March, 2008, he played his last game for St. Mirren and, at the age of 42 years 279 days, he remains the oldest player to have made an appearance in the Scottish Premier League. He stayed on as assistant manager until the end of season 2009/10.

In July 2010 he was named as the new assistant manager of Hamilton Accies, a role he held for half a season. In January

2011 he signed for Queen's Park and he reacquainted himself with playing. He appeared for that club beyond the age of forty-five. Then, in June 2011, he became the assistant manager of Queen of the South, a job he held for one season. In August 2012 he joined the coaching team at Brechin City. Alas, the arrival of new manager Ray McKinnon in October coincided with new coaches being appointed. Mr Millen had briefly been the interim manager.

In May 2013 he was appointed as an Ayr United coach, albeit that the Roberts and White management team remained intact. At the time Mark Roberts said: "I have known Andy since I was sixteen and I would trust him with my life."

Following on from the dismissal of Mark Roberts on 15th December, 2014, Mr Millen was installed as the interim manager. In the first of his three matches in charge it took a Craig Beattie goal in stoppage time to get a 2-2 draw at home to foot-of-the-table Stirling Albion. Without that timely strike we would have incurred six consecutive home league defeats (omitting Peterhead's win, since declared void).

A 3-0 defeat at Airdrie was followed by a 2-0 Stranraer win at Somerset Park on 3rd January. That result left Stranraer top and Ayr United second bottom. At that particular match it was known that the new manager was going to be named on the Monday. Brian Reid's presence in the boardroom prompted curiosity but any prospective speculation was quickly scotched when he confirmed that he would not be the new appointment.

Andy Millen was not part of the new set-up and in May 2015 he took up a job as part of the youth development at Morton. In May 2017 he took up a similar role at Kilmarnock.

Ian McCall

January 2015 –

Shortly before 6.30 p.m. on Monday, 5th January, 2015, Ian McCall was named as the new manager of Ayr United. Abraham Lincoln was attributed with saying: "You can fool all the people some of the time, and some of the people all the time but you cannot fool all the people all the time." So where is the relevance in this context? The relevance is that rumours of Billy Stark being the next Ayr boss were so rife that it was virtually accepted as fact.

Since leaving Partick Thistle in 2011, Mr McCall had been out of senior football on a working level but he had done some youth coaching and some punditry with the BBC and Radio Clyde. On being appointed to the Ayr job he said: "One of the things I remember as a player and a manager coming to Somerset Park is that it was such a difficult place to come to and get a result. The fans behind the home goal made a huge effect on the players and we need to try to get that back."

As a player he had appeared for Queen's Park, Dunfermline Athletic, Rangers, Bradford City, Dunfermline Athletic again, Dundee, Falkirk, Hamilton Accies, Happy Valley (Hong Kong), Partick Thistle and Clydebank. His managerial career to date spanned Clydebank, Morton, Airdrie, Falkirk, Dundee United, Queen of the South and Partick Thistle.

On the day after his appointment John Henry was named as his assistant. Mr Henry had played for Clydebank, Kilmarnock, Falkirk, Airdrie, St. Johnstone, Queen of the South and Dumbarton. After retiring as a player he was first team coach

Ian McCall becomes the new Ayr United manager on 5th January, 2015.

at Partick Thistle before joining Owen Coyle at Burnley where he coached the reserves. In 2010 he went with Owen Coyle to Bolton Wanderers as reserve team coach. Shortly after Coyle's dismissal in October 2012 he left Bolton. More recently he had been working with the Wigan Athletic Youth Academy.

The first game for Ian McCall was a 2-1 defeat at Brechin. In the midweek prior to the next game, both he and John Henry attended a meet-the-fans session at which they were subjected to some intense questioning. They spoke articulately and their responses were, quite sensibly, cautiously optimistic.

On 28th February a 1-0 win against Forfar Athletic was the club's first home win since 23rd August, also against Forfar. The old notion of Fortress Somerset had long since been banished anyway. Of more concern was the fact that this was not the start of a great revival. With one fixture left the foot of the table looked like this.

	P	W	D	L	F	A	Points
Ayr United	35	8	7	20	42	59	31
Stenhousemuir	35	8	5	22	40	60	29
Stirling Albion	35	3	8	24	32	82	17

The key fixtures were Forfar Athletic versus Ayr United and Stirling Albion versus Stenhousemuir. Avoiding ninth place, and therefore the relegation play-off spot, was rendered potentially difficult by Forfar sitting joint top of the league with Morton and in with a chance of winning straight promotion. It was difficult to rely on a Stenhousemuir defeat since their opposition was already doomed. In the seventh minute Forfar took the lead with a penalty and they were top of the league at this point. Six minutes later Morton reclaimed top spot by scoring against Peterhead at Cappielow. When Stenhousemuir scored at Stirling, Ayr United dropped to the play-off position.

By five o'clock it had all unravelled satisfactorily: Forfar Athletic 1 Ayr United 3 and Stirling Albion 3 Stenhousemuir 2.

The fans celebrated but a club of Ayr United's stature should not have been flirting with relegation to the fourth tier anyway.

Since being relegated in 2012 a total of twenty-three league matches had been lost at home. In the third tier this was a disgraceful statistic but the blame could not be levelled at Ian McCall. He would be judged more accurately in 2015/16.

Would the habitual false dawn manifest itself once more?

No, it was quite the opposite. On turning up for the league opener at Cliftonhill Park, the visiting supporters buoyantly expected a comfortable win over Albion Rovers. The enthusiasm dulled when the home team took the lead inside the second minute. 3-0 was the final damage. Was this an indication of what lay ahead? Happily not. The attitude of the fans was relatively restrained. This was the ground where Mark Roberts had fallen victim to an intense barrage of dissent but, this being the first league match, there was a cautious 'let's wait and see' attitude.

During the summer Mr McCall's contract had been extended until the end of 2016/17 and Nicky Devlin was named as captain at the age of twenty-one. This made him the second youngest captain in our history, the youngest being Willie McStay, who was aged nineteen when appointed the captaincy in August 1913.

After that demise at Coatbridge our next league defeat did not occur until 12th December. Fourteen consecutive league games unbeaten! None of the forlorn fans shuffling out of Cliftonhill Park (well before the end in many cases) could have foreseen this happening on the basis of that day's events. Our most formidable rival that season was Dunfermline Athletic but in fixture six we beat them 2-0 at East End Park. A 3-0 home win over Airdrie had particular relevance. The relevance was in the date, 21st November. This result meant that the club had now accrued thirty-four points. It was the same as the previous season's final total.

On Tuesday, 22nd December, 2015, Ryan Stevenson signed for Ayr United on a 28-day loan from Partick Thistle. On Thursday 21st January, 2016, he signed on until the end of the season having been released by Partick Thistle the day before. In relation to the initial loan deal Mr McCall said: "Thanks go to Partick Thistle, our main backers Bodog and to Lachlan Cameron for making the dream come true." The player commented: "If you support Barcelona you want to play for them and with me it's no different with Ayr."

Such fresh impetus was needed. A 1-0 loss at Stranraer on 2ⁿᵈ January comprised four league defeats out of the last five. Thoughts of catching leaders Dunfermline Athletic could only be entertained via outrageous optimism, a not unknown commodity in the Ayr United support, your writer included. On 12ᵗʰ March, 2016, Dunfermline's 2-0 win at Ayr made it clear to us all that promotion could only now be achieved via the play-off route.

In April consecutive 4-0 wins were recorded against Stenhousemuir then Peterhead. Only twice previously had Ayr United won consecutive matches by that precise scoreline but the feat had never been achieved in back to back away matches. More practically we were back in second place after this, a position still held after match thirty-six. In the play-off semi-finals Peterhead got brushed aside 6-2 on aggregate.

All Ian McCall had to do now for promotion was to conquer Stranraer over two legs.

Perhaps that last sentence should not have been written in such a dismissive tone. This was a club that had been bottom of the table at Christmas before embarking on resurgent form under ex-Ayr boss Brian Reid. A 1-1 draw at Stair Park in midweek only happened after Ross Docherty scored his first senior goal in the fifth minute of stoppage time. The second leg remained scoreless after 120 minutes.

Goalkeeper Greg Fleming performed heroics in the shoot-out by saving the first three he faced. The shoot-out was won and thus promotion. It was the first time Ayr United had won promotion at home since 1956. The promotions in 1959, 1966, 1969, 1988, 1997, 2009 and 2011 had all happened on away soil. On 2ⁿᵈ June, Mr McCall was awarded the trophy for League

One Manager of the Year. In July he was granted a contract covering to the end of 2017/18.

In a Championship containing clubs of the stature of Hibs (Scottish Cup holders) and Dundee United, 2016/17 stood to be a stern test. Retaining part-time football was a prospective handicap but not necessarily a prospectively fatal one. The role model was Dumbarton who had existed at this level on part-time football since 2012. Three days before the opening league game, assistant manager John Henry said that he was leaving to become a first team coach at Blackburn Rovers. Former Ayr United player Neil Scally, who had been on the coaching staff since January 2015, was immediately named as the new assistant.

In the first three league matches the team scored one goal for the loss of nine, accruing zero points in the process. Belief that things can only get better is a somewhat bleak thought process.

Bleak or not the wheel of fortune did take a favourable turn. After beating Queen of the South at Ayr on 22nd October it was possible to indulge in some favourable statistical analysis. In the previous six league games (including this one) Ayr United had gained eleven more points than Dumbarton and St. Mirren, nine more than Dunfermline Athletic, six more than Raith Rovers, five more than Queen of the South and four more than both Hibs and Morton. Over these games we had taken the same number of points as Dundee United and Falkirk.

Political pundits like to use microcosms. (If the result at Wookey Hole is representative of the rest of the country then the national picture will be...............!). In borrowing the concept of the microcosm in this context we can see that, at this time, Ayr United were as good as two other Championship clubs and better than the other seven.

Beating Hibs 2-1 at Easter Road during that run was the prompt for Ian McCall to say: "We were very disciplined defensively and scored a couple of good goals." This was proof that he was not prone to falling into the trap of reckless overstatement. Hibs had a 100% league record entering this match and the winning goal involved a move in which the ball was played the entire length of the field and into the net without an opposition player touching it. The praise of his team carried a hint of restraint. In the fickle world of football management restraint is a commendable quality which is infrequently practised. Precisely three months on from that result a draw away to St. Mirren plunged the club to ninth.

Extricating the club from the relegation area was frustratingly difficult. St. Mirren 6 Ayr United 2 on 1st April, 2017, was, most regretfully, real rather than an April Fools' Day hoax. One week later a defeat at home to Queen of the South plunged the club to the foot of the league, a position that proved irrecoverable. With complete honesty Ian McCall said: "Since starting out I have never been relegated as either a player or a manager. It's an awful feeling but I take the blame and feel the heat for it."

Of course one year earlier there was no such heat. He was revered when guiding the club to promotion and he will be revered again if he can regain any reasonable degree of success. Ayr United supporters are sometimes criticised for a 'sing when you're winning' mentality. It is unfair criticism. In re-using that word favoured in political punditry it is merely a microcosm of life.

Index

Lightning Source UK Ltd.
Milton Keynes UK
UKHW02f2230131217
314422UK00014B/1400/P